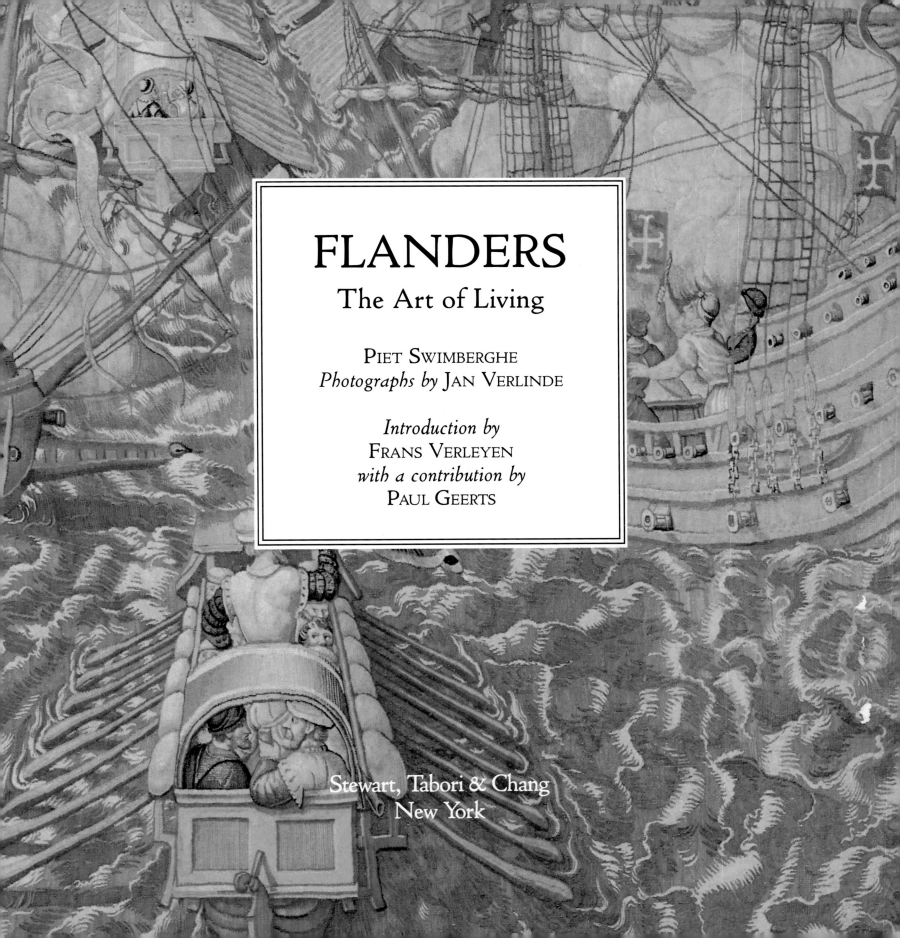

FLANDERS

The Art of Living

PIET SWIMBERGHE
Photographs by JAN VERLINDE

Introduction by
FRANS VERLEYEN
with a contribution by
PAUL GEERTS

Stewart, Tabori & Chang
New York

Chapter I

In praise of flytraps

It seemed more impressive and somehow more dignified to know everything there is to know about a single subject than to know a little about many different subjects. But now that I find myself looking at this large flea market I am beginning to wonder. My horizontal memory files contain more compassion and sympathy with others – and with myself – than a single vertical science could ever produce. Living as we do at the end of the second millennium, in the possibly lethal intoxication of progress, our capacity to marvel at things is kept alive by what we see in a Flemish market.

This greyish-green sea and constantly changing sky feature prominently in the melancholy seascapes of Louis Artan, Guillaume Vogels and Felicien Rops. They used thick blobs of paint, spreading them out on canvas to shape scudding clouds from which rain is pouring down into the sea. An art critic who preferred the French Impressionists once deprecatingly referred to their work as *peinture grasse*. The French have never understood the poetry of these "grey" painters, simply because they failed to realize that Flanders is a country of the North. Anyone wishing to catch the special atmosphere of this part of the world should walk along this arcade, part of the Thermae Palace Hotel in Ostend, one of the last Grand Hotels built on the North Sea coast. This is where James Ensor would stroll before sitting down among the dunes, a short distance away, to create his landscapes.

Page 1: This 'lion tile' from the De Knock workshop has been modelled after typically eighteenth-century Flemish tiles.

Page 2: This superb Brussels tapestry is the showpiece of the Mechelen town hall. It represents Charles V's naval battle off Tunis.

Page 4: Flanders' most spectacular ceiling adorns a loft in Ghent.

This is the symbolic border between the Northern and the Southern Netherlands, between Holland and Belgium. To the left is the Dutch town of Sluis, once an outpost of Bruges, hidden behind ditches and rows of poplars keeping watch like so many soldiers. The comparison is apt, for at the end of the sixteenth century the Netherlands were split in two. It is hard to imagine that this dike was once an Iron Curtain separating Protestants and Catholics. On both sides massive fortifications were built with enormous earthworks.

For generations contacts were kept to a minimum. But that time is now long past. This boundary post is merely an antique curiosity.

(next page)
This fine orthodox monastery can be found in the Pervijze polders.

In just two centuries a complete town was built on the banks of this river, the Reie. The builders had to start from scratch, for like most other Flemish towns Bruges has hardly any Roman roots.
To the left, beyond the trees, are ostentatious merchant houses. They used to be simple workshops where masons sculpted this entire panorama. For this is Steenhouwersdijk – the stonemasons' dike – where all of Bruges' historical buildings, such as the Cloth Hall with its Belfry and the City Hall looming up behind the roof tops, were made stone by stone. It was a long time ago and yet it does not seem an eternity, for relatively few things have changed. It is easy to imagine ships mooring here, loaded with bricks and mortar.

I AM STANDING IN THE MIDDLE OF a market square in Flanders. It is a large square, tapering off to one short side. This trapezoid shape is a gradually developed compromise between the long-forgotten Celtic triangle and the exact, all too rational square of the Renaissance.

The fronts of the houses display a mixture of historical styles. Flemish towns are highly eclectic, having learned to breathe with many different pairs of lungs. They have inhaled Gallo-Roman, Spanish, Italian, French and Austrian air. A century ago another, Belgian component was added, consisting of an indeterminate mixture of Art Nouveau and kitsch. Kitsch is a nineteenth-century word, derived from *kitschen*, which means 'hastily brushing up wet rubbish'. That, of course, is precisely what incompetent dabblers do. As producers of phoney art they are indispensable, however, for what use would real art be to the *hoi polloi* ?

Behind those fronts the gentry used to live. Today, they have mostly been replaced by the middle classes, who, ever since the French Revolution, have been an essential political buffer between an interfering, meddlesome government and the union-controlled working class. Here, on the market square, the middle classes are represented by a shop selling curtains, three different banks, a Chinese restaurant, two pavement cafés and a house belonging to a solicitor, a splendid building radiating the tranquillity of the law in a turbulent world full of inheritances and alimonies.

Today, the square is full of people. Under a blue sky market stalls have been set up, selling all sorts of bric-a-brac. During the summer months every town of any description organizes at least one of these open-air flea markets. No-one knows where all the secondhand dealers come from, but they seem to be well-organized, run vans to transport their wares and follow a regular schedule. One Sunday they take their underground economy to Nieuwpoort in the west of the country, the next to Maasmechelen in the east.

I stroll among the stalls with their flamboyantly offered wares. Young, plebeian sales girls in frayed jeans sit on the wide pavement. No-one seems to supervise them or order them about. Have they finally gained their freedom ? Behind a row of wooden cages men selling tame parakeets are loitering. Flea markets like these portray Flanders in its many different and sometimes improbable aspects. This particular market is a symphony of discarded objects, including furniture, mirrors, crucifixes, gadgets, playing cards, earrings, rosary beads, books and kitchen utensils. A careful observer can learn much here about the true behaviour of his fellow-men, about their good deeds and their sins.

Precious antiques are, fortunately, rarely for sale on Flemish flea markets. What they do offer is an excellent view of the tangible remains, the insignificant vestiges, of two or three earlier generations. They teach us humility when we study the china angels, chamberpots, brass doorhandles and mouldering wireless sets that were banned from the houses where we grew up. More expressively than any museum they tell the story of ideas and life-styles rejected and cast out just before and after World War II.

I notice a small collection of charcoal drawings, mounted on dirty cardboard and put behind glass in gilt frames. They carry the signature of a certain Albert Devocht. The powerful lines with which he rendered his coloured landscapes betray his confidence. The waves of the North Sea, frothing and seething dramatically, break on dunes resembling tall Alps. Cattle like small mammoths are placidly grazing in the flat polders. A river, probably the Scheldt near Terneuzen or Sint-Amands, winds its way through a purplish blue 'meadow symphony', the title of this work. From the louvers of an indeterminate churchtower a wavy ribbon

Every Flemish town partakes of Rubensian Baroque. Even the fronts of simple houses are exuberantly ornamented. In Ghent especially you will be tempted to look up time after time at the gables of the houses lavishly adorned with sculpted ornaments. This beauty can be found in Ghent's Patershol quarter.

Antwerp at dawn (pages 18-19). The sun is rising from behind the churchtowers. A metropolis like Antwerp never really goes to sleep, of course, for the docks stay awake day and night. But seen from the left bank of the Scheldt the old town is as peaceful as a painting by Johannes Vermeer.

inscribed with musical notes emerges, like the billowing clothes of an angel. Underneath is a text from which I can decipher the words *zingende heimat*, the singing country. A woman pushing a pram, who looks like a devoted village schoolteacher or a welfare worker for the elderly, buys the picture for the price of four packets of cigarettes.

Inevitably, Albert Devocht and other artists of his ilk are hard put to find scenes of dramatic grandeur in the Flemish countryside. Apart from some hills of 300 feet or so high, invariably called 'mountains', Flanders is as flat as a pancake. The horizon is merely a straight line across a sheet of drawing paper. There is not much artists can do with that. Basically, they have just two options – either they will invent a non-existing landscape, with imaginary moors rising up like some kind of Flemish Vosges among mighty streams and rivers, or they will go in search of anything breaking the monotony of the skyline, such as ramshackle cottages, village towers, Gothic churches, barbed wire across barren snow-covered steppes or distant, solitary elmtrees. Jacques Brel did much the same thing in his songs. He, too, helped the myth of *le plat pays* along, the flat country that in the minds of the people is more turbulent than it can ever be in reality.

A large crowd saunters by, in search of the jetsam and flotsam of this century and the past. A remarkably large number of the objects for sale are associated with popular beliefs, religious faith or the policy of the Catholic church. Worn missals display the *confiteor Deo omnipotenti*, the confession of sins, in large capitals. A cardboard box full of Confirmation pictures still smells of the pious dreams of newly initiated twelve-year-old girls in white satin dresses, their curls hidden under a cloud of transparant tulle – images of veiled virginity. Sacred hearts under glass covers tell the mysterious epic of the god with his bloodied chest from which

flames are flashing like lightning. Blue statuettes of Our Lady of Lourdes in earthenware grottoes are ecstatically looking up to a heavenly light, inaccessible to earth-bound mortals. A sturdy crucifix crowns a model of Mount Calvary carved from oak and shaped like a skull.

Near a pub called *Patria* is Anton's stall. He sells old watches and mechanical toys, superannuated cameras and bottles of perfume. Anton is actually from Holland – he prices his goods in Dutch guilders – but he went to live in Flemish Eeklo some time ago and has by now mastered the local dialect. Last year I asked him where he got his treasures from, but that turned out to be a professional secret. My curiosity raised his suspicions, as if I were pl⋯⋯⋯ ⋯e Fort Knox of secondhand wares.

This time his unknown source has supplied him with a musical box, a little drum major done up in Napoleonic costume. This trinket from an Ostend workshop is too expensive for me, but perhaps I can get him to reduce the price of that silver hunter and chain. I have bought several of such watches from him before, which should automatically entitle me to a discount.

Anton presses the button, flips open the solid lid and eyes my reaction with interest. To market vendors I must be an ignoramus, an easy victim. At first I fail to see that the inside of the lid is decorated with a miniature painting – an elegantly dressed aristocrat is taking his advantage of a frightened chambermaid, whose many skirts he has lifted to steal a look at her suspenders. Painted pornography for the nineteenth-century Antwerp aristocracy, furtive evil in the private rooms of the gentry, the gross subjection of a servant girl, the social question in the guise of lasciviousness – these things are only too familiar to the Flemish.

Seen through a magnifying glass every detail of the crime scene becomes clear. The nobleman is sitting in

20

a corner of his sofa, his doublet and velvet breeches unbuttoned. Behind him is a bulging chest of drawers, with conspicuously on top a gleaming clock next to a statuette of a nun (St Theresa of Avila perhaps?) under a glass bell. The servant girl is dramatically poised for flight; her lace headdress has already slipped onto her shoulders. But all is in vain – he has got hold of her, his exaggeratedly large hands pulling at her clothes while his horn-rimmed spectacles fall to the floor.

The miniaturist who portrayed this lewd scene on a surface of roughly a square inch added a highly symbolic touch: the clock inside the watch represents an obsession with time ticking away the years of voluptuousness and greed. The social psychology of Flanders, insofar as anyone can understand it, may well have the notion of *time* as its main element. An awareness of the right time to do things, a set pattern of work and relaxation, a tendency to feel guilty when lazing about on Sundays, the seasons dictating the kind of work that is to be done and alternately promising plenty or threatening scarcity, the legally ordained holidays and festivals (fairs included), the periodical materialization of the reproductive urge, as often as not involving adulterous desires – all this is consciously or unconsciously part of the collective memory of all those who have had their roots in Flanders for at least a century.

To remind us of the passing of time on a grander scale, of what we call history, the market square has been graced with a statue of a national hero, a historical totem pole around which the crowds visiting the flea market assemble in perfect harmony, carrying the smell of hamburgers with them. But other things besides erecting memorials keep the collective memory alive. One of the vendors sells relics from colonial Congo. He has been selling them for years, perhaps ever since the day he was driven from this Belgian tropical paradise.

His wares include a small statue of a genuine-looking Congolese warrior, probably made in the amateurish bronze workshop of a mission school in Katanga.

Perhaps it is more than a coincidence that his neighbour is Rudi, a mustachioed and tattooed man who is accompanied by a few lethargic punk girls. He sells old copies of *Signal*, the journal of the German Wehrmacht, and other military items from the thirties and forties. Rudi's business thrives on the not yet completely digested memory of the German occupation, when many Flemish nationalists collaborated with the Nazi regime and were punished afterwards by Belgian courts, which in their patriotic zeal often took a bigoted view of the confusion and weakness that sometimes besets a nation. Here we see the relics of war in all their trite banality – glossy pictures of Hitler, carefully concealing the Führer's paunch and other physical imperfections, gas masks, belts, helmets, defused handgrenades, medals and epaulettes, ration vouchers, regulations issued by the German *Kommandantur* and dealing with blackouts or closing hours in German and Flemish.

Hardly less uncanny are the various objects that used to help people get on with their daily lives. Thermometers and barometers show the vagaries of the weather, now or in future, in neat copperplate along tiny, luminescent tubes or spirals of mercury. Brass microscopes rest in mahogany chests. Flytraps that had to be filled with sugar water in order to tempt the insects to drown themselves testify to the old adage that a little cunning goes a long way. Hair-thin needles oscillate on kitchen-scales or scales used for the *pharmacie*, the family pharmacopoeia.

The medical gear in particular includes quite a lot of mysterious horrors. Medical corsets, artificial limbs, bedpans, syringes used for enemas, herbal preparations, forceps and heavy stethoscopes stir in me a vague

Everywhere in Belgium socialists and liberals built workman's clubs of surprisingly modern design. Here we are on the roof of the former liberal workman's club in Antwerp, built in 1901. It is situated in Zuid, a district which came into being in 1864 after the demolition of an immense castle. Docks were built, as well as a beautiful museum, which is the main landmark in this part of the city.

fear of the authoritarian medicine practised in my long-gone youth. Doctors would often hurt you then, removing tonsils from the throats of schoolchildren gagging on the awful smell of chloroform.

It is more fun to browse among the remains of another lost world, that of pubs and hostelries which have long since been closed. Advertisements for long-forgotten brands of beer on enamelled signs, now worth quite a lot of money. Lemonade bottles with narrow necks and a glass marble for a stopper. Azure siphons with small levers you had to squeeze to add fizzy soda water to syrup or Scotch. Glasses of every imaginable shape, including pint-sized tankards with solid handles and goblets with the brand names of beers engraved or painted on them. German wineglasses on green stems, absinthe carafes shaped like a series of rings put on top of each other, small gin glasses with heavy feet filled with air bubbles, coffee filters of blackened silver. The archeology of Flemish pub life also includes the yellowed posters explaining the drinking laws in letters so small you cannot read them with the naked eye.

Last but not least, there are the increasingly rare pub tables made of indestructible elm with their twisted legs. They show signs of prolonged abuse: damp stains, scratches, knife cuts, ink (from love letters perhaps ?), grease, nicked edges. Their size must have corresponded to a spontaneous need, for most of them are 35 inches long, 20 inches wide and 30 inches tall. The ones that deviate from these measurements do not partake of the harmony of the spheres. They create an undefinable sense of discomfort, as if the proper space required by two tipplers is determined by a hidden natural law.

Much the same thing goes for *escritoires*, those complicated writing desks with their many drawers and pigeonholes, their slots for putting letters in, their hinged writing surfaces where one may ply one's pen-

manship. The distance between those writing surfaces and one's knees is crucial in determining whether these desks can be used with any comfort at all. A mere inch either way may be decisive. Old desks often prove to be too small. Our ancestors were on average four inches shorter than we are, as old army uniforms show. Most escritoires are therefore only fit to be put in a corner of the living room, where they can be decorative in the yellow light of a lampshade.

At the book stall I buy, with a twinge of nostalgia, a ten-volume set of science books for young people, published in the good old fifties. These books instructed you how to lower – or to raise ? – the level of liquid in a glass by freezing a spoonful of water and then throwing the ice cube back in. They showed you how to balance two forks, stuck into a cork, by putting a needle into the cork and poising it on the rim of a full glass. They explained that a fly would look much larger if you looked at it through a small hole in a piece of cardboard. They contained magic squares, each divided into nine parts, that would help you do stunning mathematical tricks by using simple sets of numerals. And they included the first photographs of the planet Jupiter, printed on glossy paper.

Much as I used to love these books and the mysteries they unveiled so effortlessly – the weight of a chicken feather, the elasticity of marbles, the shape of an aircraft's wings, the specific gravity of salad oil – I did not become a research chemist or a physicist, but a writer. There have been times when I regretted this. It seemed more impressive and somehow more dignified to know everything there is to know about a single subject than to know a little about many different subjects. But now that I find myself looking at this large flea market I am beginning to wonder. My horizontal memory files contain more compassion and sympathy with others – and with myself – than a single vertical

The funny tower of the Vooruit festival hall strikes a playful note in the Ghent townscape, dominated by three medieval towers, those of St Michael's (left), the Belfry and St Bavo's.

science could ever produce. Living as we do at the end of the second millennium, in the possibly lethal intoxication of progress, our capacity to marvel at things is kept alive by what we see in a Flemish market.

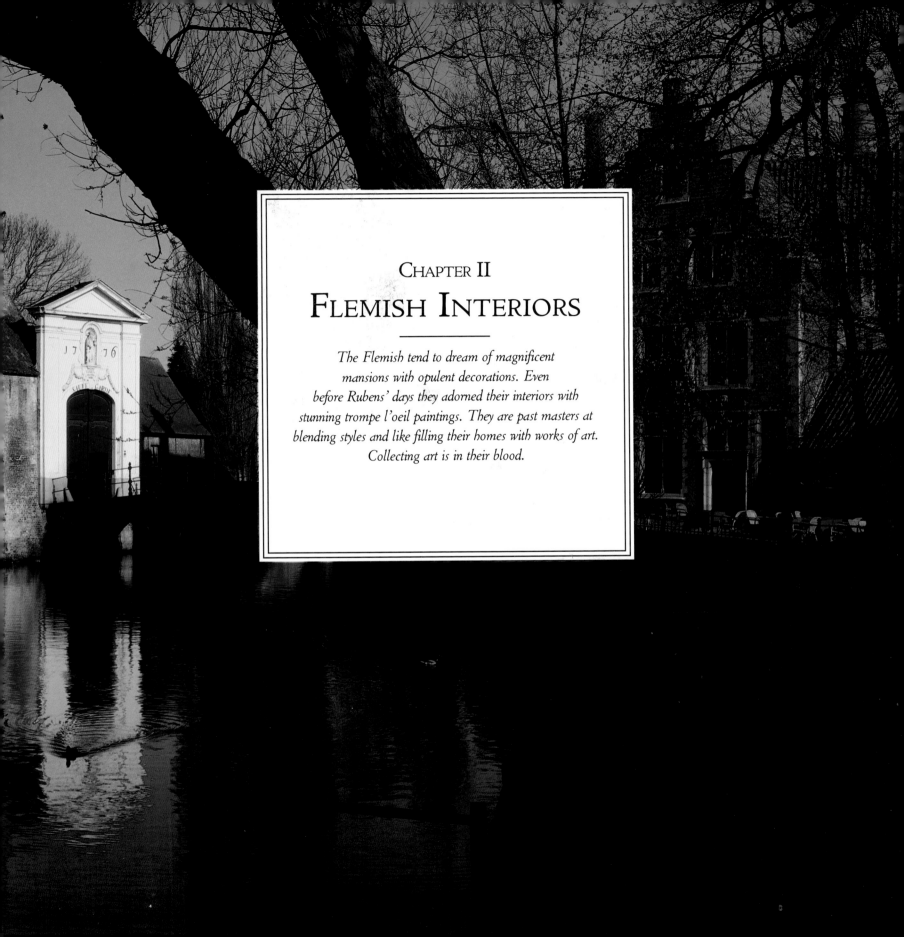

CHAPTER II
FLEMISH INTERIORS

The Flemish tend to dream of magnificent
mansions with opulent decorations. Even
before Rubens' days they adorned their interiors with
stunning trompe l'oeil paintings. They are past masters at
blending styles and like filling their homes with works of art.
Collecting art is in their blood.

IN THE
FOOTSTEPS
OF JAN
VAN EYCK

―――

Bruges is a city steeped in the past. At the foot of the Church of Our Lady (above) you enter the world of one of Jan van Eyck's paintings. The slender brick spire, the old bridges and the medieval mansions have all remained untouched by time. Autumn is the best season to go for a stroll along these old streets and squares.

When in Ghent or Bruges the first thing to do is to visit a museum. It is a good idea to start with the Flemish Primitives to get an impression of what Flanders is like. This fragment of Jan van Eyck's Adoration of the Mystic Lamb *shows a unique view of Ghent. At one time Flemish towns were teeming with curtain walls, step-gables and houses with wooden fronts.*

STROLLING THROUGH BRUGES or nearby Damme you sometimes feel as if you have magically entered the world of one of Jan Van Eyck's paintings. Caught in a reverie, I can see sailors unloading wine casks from wooden cog-ships moored along the quays of the Spiegelrei in Bruges. On the hump-backed Spiegel Bridge – strikingly similar to the curved back of an old walrus – elderly women are selling fresh milk and eggs to passers-by. The small square in front of the toll house is alive with the shouts of wine-tasting tradesmen. Everywhere foreign merchants dressed in exotic finery walk by. This is what Bruges must have looked like in the past. But now this part of the city is quiet and peaceful.

It is great fun to let your imagination run free and recall the former glories of this part of Bruges, where every brick is steeped in history. The sights and vistas seem to have been lifted straight from a painting by one of the Flemish Primitives. Even the trading houses of the Florentines, the Genoese and the Basques have escaped the wrecker's ball – a poignant reminder of what might have been.

Seen from the top of a churchtower, Flemish cities look more like ports than anything else – water, quays and docks are everywhere. The houses crowd each other, pressing together like a fleet of ships at anchor. The saddle-roofed buildings facing the streets and alleys seem almost like medieval merchantmen.

The twisting streets show that most Flemish towns do not have their roots in the ancient past. Unlike the cities of France, many of which go back to Roman times, the cities of Flanders sprang up from the soil, and this has determined their character. They were created by merchants who had settled on riverbanks near an abbey or a castle. Their mercantile origins still show quite clearly in the ostentatious buildings, vying with each other in size and stature. In the twelfth century the rich merchant-princes of Ghent were so busy trying to outdo each other by building taller houses than their neighbours that the archbishop decided to intervene. Archeologists have discovered the reason for the prelate's exasperation – many medieval mansions were so tall that they towered over the roofs of the churches, and this could not, of course, be tolerated. In addition, many houses were provided with fortified towers and had such thick walls that they put the local castle to shame. Naturally, such effrontery was frowned upon.

Still, all this display of pride and wealth did create beautiful cities. Ghent and Bruges are simply teeming with imposing medieval buildings. But even though the two cities are not far distant, their houses look completely different. Ghent, situated on the Scheldt, imported blue stone from Tournai. Bruges had to make do with clay bricks. The city is an ode to brickbuilding. Many façades are decorated with subtle brick tracery incorporating the basic shapes of High Gothic. Each façade has its own distinctive style with decorative cramp irons and stone tablets. They are delightful to look at.

Step-gables are a typical feature of many Flemish houses. The oldest, going back almost eight hundred years, can be found in Ghent. Each individual step is covered with a small tile roof. But the most recent step-gables date from as late as the eighteenth century. Unlikely as it may seem, architects simply carried on constructing the same façades for five hundred years, completely ignoring changes in fashion. Even more impressive than the ubiquitous step-gables is a type of façade known as a curtain wall – a prime example of ostentation, because they are false fronts which are far taller than the buildings they hide. They are often crenellated, much like a castle. Some Ghent houses with curtain walls are shown in one of the panels of Jan van Eyck's *Adoration of the Mystic Lamb*. Sadly, most of

Five centuries ago the painter Jan van Eyck (above) would have been standing among a crowd of Basques, Catalans, Portuguese and Lombards. This small square in Bruges, which now bears his name, used to be the bustling centre of the medieval port. It was also the financial heart of the city, for the world's earliest Exchange was nearby. The old merchant houses along the quays seem remarkably austere, despite their dignified air. They are probably former warehouses that were transformed into residential buildings when the port declined.

This mysterious building in Bruges (above) has a romantic name: the Black House. The origin of the name seems to be unknown, although it is true that the façade had a dark colour before it was restored a few years ago. This magnificent example of Flemish brick Gothic has one of the finest curtain walls in the Low Countries. The builder may have wanted to show off, as the façade is much larger and taller than the house itself.

All Flemish towns used to be water-logged. Among the network of rivers and canals saddle-roofed dwelling houses and warehouses were built. When you look down on them from the top of a tower, they seem like small ships moored alongside each other.

these façades have now gone. In Bruges, however, a number of beautiful curtain walls have been preserved, particularly the huge one of the Black House, which is a true landmark. This tall building soars up like a medieval skyscraper.

Many buildings in Flemish cities were destroyed, being either pulled down or modernized. But in Bruges much has been preserved, not just individual structures but the ensemble as well. This fortunate state of affairs is largely due to the efforts of a number of English expatriates who settled in Bruges in the mid-nineteenth century. Some of them were associates or followers of Augustus Pugin, the famous English architect who initiated the Gothic revival. To them, Bruges seemed like the setting of a medieval romance. They greatly admired our antiquities and taught us to reevaluate the Middle Ages, helping to restore historical buildings in the process. Thus the English were indirectly responsible for the Flemish heritage movement. It is thanks to them that the dreamy atmosphere of the past has been kept alive in Bruges. Let us hope it will remain with us for a long time to come.

Bruges was unharmed by wars and the Industrial Revolution. Factory chimneys are missing from its skyline, but church towers abound. In the centre is the Belfry, with the Romanesque St. Salvator Tower, surrounded by scaffolding, to its right. The tower of the Church of Our Lady is the pride of the city. It soars to a height of 400 feet and was built around 1300. St. Anna's Church in the foreground is resting like an elderly lady in a bed of town houses. There are also many smaller towers, belonging to medieval mansions.

In Northern Europe the transition from Gothic to Classical architecture was not an easy process. The first Renaissance buildings were constructed by craftsmen whose heart was in the Middle Ages, as the Gothic contours of Bruges' Record Office, completed in 1537, make abundantly clear. The Renaissance did not only transform architecture in the Low Countries, it also spelled the end for the master builders, craftsmen who had learned their trade on the building sites of large churches. They were replaced by a new type of builders, known as architects, who looked to illustrations in books for inspiration.
It was a long time before the new architectural concepts were fully accepted. In the meantime a strange mixture of styles was used – more proof that eclecticism is part of the Flemish way of life.

SOMETIMES I WONDER why people have stopped painting dates on the front of their homes. Are we perhaps frightened by the passage of time ? Or are architects and builders afraid that this practice will make their buildings seem to age faster ? For many centuries Flemish houses proudly proclaimed to all and sundry when they were built. Putting a date on a façade literally represented the finishing touch. Some people were satisfied with a stone tablet set between two windows, but others who were keen to show off opted for imposing wrought-iron numerals. Even the smallest houses thus became witnesses of the past. Streets take on a different aspect when you know in what year the houses were built. Whenever I see two almost identical façades I begin to speculate about the story behind this similarity of design. Could it be that two neighbours tried to outdo each other ? Pride and a display of wealth were often motivating forces when building a house – extra steps would be added to step-gables simply to impress the people next door. The various dates also make clear that it took only a very short time for some façades to undergo a complete transformation. If the local baker, for instance, had the front of his shop redesigned the other shopkeepers in the street would soon follow suit. In this way cities and towns would gradually change their appearance, with different styles of architecture smoothly overlapping each other. Architectural styles usually changed far less abruptly than they do today, because builders were less keen on innovation than we are. As late as the seventeenth century stately homes were entirely medieval in appearance. Many ornamental odds and ends were inspired by Italian Baroque, but nobody tampered with the basic layout.

At one time a mixture of no fewer than three different styles prevailed in Flanders – Gothic, Renaissance and Baroque. Eclecticism has always been part of the Flemish way of life. In the eighteenth century Dutch bell-gabled houses were built next to houses with French mansard roofs. In the nineteenth century styles became even more garbled; nowhere else in Europe can such a confusion of architectural designs be found as in Flanders. It was the Renaissance that set this eclecticism in motion, and for an obvious reason – it took us Northerners a long time to understand the art of the South. Architects who had been used to pointed arches had to make a considerable effort to familiarize themselves with the principles involved in building along classical lines. But that was not all. Romanesque and Gothic architecture had gradually found its way into Flanders along the major rivers, the Scheldt, Meuse and Rhine. But the concepts of the Renaissance entered Flanders through its ports. The new fashion spread because shrewd merchants, conscious of its commercial value, eagerly seized the opportunity and created a flourishing trade in tapestries, prints, musical instruments and other luxury goods, particularly in Antwerp. It took more than a century before the rebirth of the Renaissance had taken a firm hold. Surprising, really, considering that even in the fifteenth century a city like Bruges had a large population of Spaniards and Italians who were familiar with the Renaissance. By the end of the fifteenth century the focus of economic activity shifted from Bruges to Antwerp and Mechelen. Even then it took almost another generation before the first Renaissance building was constructed, a wing of Margaret of Austria's palace in Mechelen. But just like the Records Office in Bruges, the palace combines a classical front with a purely medieval soul. The first truly authentic Renaissance building in Flanders is Antwerp's renowned city hall.

Only a few 'modern' Renaissance buildings have been preserved. Much has been lost and soon after the final separation of the Low Countries in the seventeenth century Flanders entered the period of high Baroque with the amazing Rubens.

With this façade (left) the Renaissance really took off. This is the Antwerp City Hall, built from 1561 to 1565 by Cornelis Floris de Vriendt, a Flemish painter and architect who lived in Italy. The City Hall was a model of Renaissance architecture in the Low Countries.

St Carolus Borromeus' Church in Antwerp (right), was built by Pieter Huyssens less than a hundred years later. It is one of the finest examples of Italian Baroque in Flanders. Hidden away in a corner of St Veerleplein in Ghent is the most beautiful Baroque structure of the Low Countries. It seems odd that something as commonplace as a fish market (below) should have been so opulently adorned. But it is not really all that strange, for this portal stands near the place where the Rivers Scheldt and Leie meet. They are symbolised by figures flanking the window above the entrance. The portal is, of course, crowned by a statue of Neptune holding his trident, as if he had just stepped out of a painting by Rubens.

In the past fortunes were spent on the decorations of façades. The sculptors of Ghent were kept very busy indeed, as virtually every façade was adorned with numerals, stone tablets and ornaments. The most elegant houses are on Graslei and Korenlei. This charming bell-gable (right) belongs to the Guild House of the Unfree Boatmen. It was designed by Bernard de Wilde and dates from 1739. You can see the masculine Baroque style turning smoothly into feminine Rococo.

GUESTS OF RUBENS

—

N O INHABITANT of Antwerp can fail to be aware of Rubens, for the city is saturated with his presence. Every single stone is steeped in his spirit. When you enter St Carolus Borromeus' Church you will at once find him there. His influence is visible in the shapes and contours of the tiniest details. It almost seems as if he brought this church – containing dozens of his paintings – with him from Rome, for it is purely Italian. Rubens loved Rome and almost decided to settle there permanently. It was Rubens who, together with the Spanish of an earlier era, created Antwerp's mediterranean atmosphere. This peculiar aspect of Antwerp immediately strikes the visitor strolling around the city centre and noticing the many enclosed patios at the back of the houses. The vivid colours, the impression of disorder and the somewhat casual attitude of the population betray the city's southern roots. Rubens would never have felt happy in calvinist Amsterdam or among the French, because neither the French nor the Dutch have absorbed southern Baroque as thoroughly as the Flemish. In Rubens' lifetime, during the first half of the seventeenth century, Flanders was more than ever the northernmost outpost of southern Europe.

More of that southern influence remains than we tend to think. The Flemish still love the South, and this is reflected in their way of life. Their language may have northern origins, but their cuisine and temperament are deeply rooted in the South. Rubens, too, was inspired by southern Europe. His fascination with Spain and Italy may well have been the reason why he became a diplomat, a profession which enabled him to travel. His art allowed him to enter Caravaggio's world, if not in reality, then at least in his mind. I suspect that, like Michelangelo Caravaggio, he would rather have achieved fame in Rome than in the more temperate

North. His Baroque paintings and his magnificent home, now a delightful museum, are an expression of the Italianate universe he created. Thus he could imagine himself to be in Rome, even when he stayed in the heart of Antwerp.

His attempts to create another, Italian world have been quite successful, as any visitor to his garden will confirm. Sit down in the shade of the pavilion under a blue sky and enjoy the long rows of citrus trees lining the path to the portico. What I find most attractive about the pavilion are its small, slightly tilted pillars. It seems as fragile as a house of cards but it is rather more solid, for it has been here since Rubens' time. I think it is one of the most delightful mementoes that Rubens brought back from his travels; you would swear that he took it with him from some Florentine *piazza*. Rubens himself clearly liked it, for it figures prominently in a portrait of himself and his second wife, Hélène Fourment. The Flemish-Italian garden of Rubens' house was recently redesigned with many flowerbeds set among low yew hedges and restored to what it must have looked like in the days of this great artist. The garden offers a magnificent view of the portico, the most original Baroque structure of the Low Countries. It is topped by statues of Hermes and Athena, watching over commerce and art – no doubt a jocular reference to Rubens' flourishing painting business.

Pieter Paul Rubens worshipped Antiquity. To compensate for the lack of Greek and Roman remains in Flanders he decorated the walls of his palace with reconstructions of classical paintings. Despite the overwhelming beauty of the rear façade it is only a weak reflection of what it used to be. Originally the entire façade was covered by a huge trompe l'oeil on a blank wall, creating a deceptive impression of sculptured architecture. It was a fitting embellishment of a painter's home. Sadly, the architect who carried out a pains-

taking reconstruction of the house earlier this century missed the point entirely. He had the original façade, by that time plastered over, cut away in an attempt to discover the remnants of the sculptured surface. Nothing was found, of course, since the decoration consisted only of a thin coat of paint which was destroyed in the process. In addition, the façade was redone in stonework relief. Even so, the result is very attractive.

The reconstructed façade contrasts starkly with the interior, which is far less monumental. The living rooms are grouped around the courtyard. Some rooms contain sculpted fireplaces and have walls hung with gilt leather, an early type of wall decoration. In the seventeenth and eighteenth centuries Mechelen was the most important centre for the manufacture of this precursor of wallpaper. These leather wall coverings with their scenes in relief were very popular among the rich, who used them as a backdrop to the many oak cupboards and oriental carpets in their homes.

Rubens' atelier is huge, certainly for an artist of his time. In this large room he painted most of his masterpieces, together with fellow-artists like Anthony van Dyck and Frans Snyders. It is exciting to think how many paintings were created here. One floor up there is another large room where Rubens' pupils worked, mass-producing paintings to order.

At the far end of the building is Rubens' private picture gallery, a place where he could withdraw and where visitors were only rarely allowed. His picture gallery was a mirror of the world. It was also a miniature copy of Rome, for annexed to it is an apsidal Pantheon where busts of contemporaries and classical artists are displayed. Rubens had quite a large collection of classical art and antiques. A head of Seneca is prominently displayed. Like many other humanists of his time, Rubens deeply admired this Roman philosopher.

Rubens also owned many coins, cameos and other

precious objects. His collection even included an Egyptian mummy, as well as many paintings by old and modern masters. Inevitably, the works of major Italian painters such as Titian, Tintoretto, Veronese and Raphael were well represented. Eventually his collection became so huge that he had to buy several small houses adjacent to his garden in order to be able to store all his objects. His library was another prized possession. Thanks to the account he kept with his friend Moretus, the publisher, we have a fairly good idea of what it contained, including a remarkably large number of architectural treatises. Don't be deceived into thinking, however, that Rubens bought all these books and art objects simply because he enjoyed beautiful things. There is no doubt that his collection was as much an investment as anything else, reminding us of the truth that there is nothing new under the sun.

From beyond the long table Rubens sneaks a glance at his visitors. This is one of his rare self-portraits. The room has been refurnished in line with the fashions of Rubens' age, as exemplified by the heavy oak furniture, the marble floor and the gilt leather wall coverings (left). Rubens was passionately interested in architecture. His house brings the heritage of great architects such as Vitruvius, Serlio and Scamozzi back to life.

This is Rubens' private picture gallery, the most intimate part of the house where only his closest friends were invited. Rubens was a keen collector, owning paintings by contemporary artists as well as many antiques, including an Egyptian mummy and a series of Roman busts. He displayed his collection of busts in an apsidal Pantheon, modelled after the one in Rome (above).

Rubens' house is a trip to nostalgia. The era of Baroque comes back to life here in the tiniest detail. The stained-glass windows of the house are an excellent example (left).

Wandering through this beautiful house you gradually come under the spell of this great artist. Not just because of the flamboyant architecture and the many old paintings, but also because of the generous light penetrating every room. The subtle play of light and shadow has never been better expressed than by Baroque.

42

The Flemish-Italian Renaissance garden of Rubens' house was recently restored. The restoration was based on his painting A Walk in the Garden from 1630, a superb marriage portrait of the artist with his second wife Hélène Fourment and his son Nicolaas. This beautiful garden pavilion is prominently displayed in the painting. On a summer day, standing in front of it, you can easily imagine yourself to be in a Florentine piazza.

RENDEZ-VOUS
WITH
MOZART

—

Flanders prospered in the mid-eighteenth century. Large mansions with magnificent gardens full of arbours and bowers were built in every Flemish town. This bonbonnière *can be found in the garden of the Arents House in Bruges, now the home of the Brangwyn Museum. The house has a portal in Egyptian style.*

IN SEPTEMBER 1763 Leopold Mozart and his children Nannerl and Wolfgang spent a few days in Ghent. Isn't it wonderful to think that young Mozart was then one of our countrymen, since at the time Flanders was ruled by Austria ? The Flemish have been fortunate in that they have been ruled by so many other nations, including the French, the Spanish, the Austrians and the Dutch. Many foreign cultures have inspired us, as the unique heritage of our architecture shows. In Mozart's age – the eighteenth century – foreign influences had reached the height of refinement. But if I should have met Leopold Mozart, the famous composer's father, I would certainly have quarreled with him. He thought Ghent was a dull city, whereas in my opinion it is the most beautiful eighteenth-century city in Flanders.

The much-travelled Mozart family arrived in Flanders from Paris, on their way to the Dutch court at The Hague. They had been received at the court in Brussels, but they were disappointed about their reception there – prince Charles of Lorraine was a popular ruler, but he preferred hunting and dining to music. Perhaps this still rankled when Leopold Mozart sat down to report his adventures to his patron. In the letter he wrote he said that he had enjoyed Brussels and Leuven more than Ghent. He had particularly liked the lively university town of Leuven. The Mozarts had been deeply impressed by the street lighting of Brussels – they had never before seen the darkness of night driven away by so many lights. Leopold also found words of praise for the excellent highways – according to him their carriage had moved so smoothly that it seemed as if the roads were covered by carpets. But Ghent, he said, was a large, dreary modern city with some old monuments and many new buildings. Perhaps he had a point after all. To the Mozarts Ghent was simply too modern and mundane. They had already seen quite a

lot of modern buildings in the French style. Besides, in 1763 Ghent was a beehive of activity with construction and reconstruction going on everywhere. The charming step-gables were being pulled down to be replaced by monumental façades with plasterwork painted in brilliant colours. The city must have looked much like Brussels today – a jumble of building trenches, scaffolding, cranes and ships transporting building materials. Chaos prevailed everywhere. All over the city magnificent *hôtels de maître* were being built. The Mozarts lodged in one of these mansions, the Hôtel Saint-Sébastien on Kouter, Ghent's central square. Today the elegant façades of the Hoofdwacht and the Hôtel Falligan recall the former picturesqueness of this square. Even now this is where the burghers of Ghent will go for a walk on Sundays among the flower booths and the oyster stalls. In Mozart's time the city theatre was situated on Kouter as well. It was the focus of Ghent society life, where actors from Paris and Italy came to perform plays by Beaumarchais, Molière and Pergolesi. Ghent at that time was a fashionable city where *redoutes*, or masked balls, were being held every week during the winter months. Leopold may have found all this glitter and glamour a bit too *nouveau riche* for his taste. The streets of the city were full of pretentious upstarts displaying their wealth, much of which had been earned by selling cloth to foreign armies. In the early nineteenth century Ghent had become so rich that a new opera house was built. It was recently restored to its original splendour. Flanders has of late seen a renewed interest in opera, thanks to people like Gerard Mortier, the former manager of the Munt Theatre in Brussels, and many music theatres have now been restored to their former glory, including Antwerp's sublime Bourla Theatre.

Mozart would have been surprised by the opulent furnishings of the Ghent opera house. They were the

work of Paris decorators with lyrical names like Humanité-René Philastre and Charles-Antoine Cambon. Ghent used to be a very French city. Architects and interior decorators used French models, devoutly studying the works of Marot, Blondel and Boffrand and visiting the French capital to keep up-to-date with the latest fashions. Bernard de Wilde and David 't Kindt, Ghent's two leading architects, were fascinated by the French *façon de vivre*. Their Rococo designs with their heavy cornices, luxuriant figures and many gilt surfaces are typically Baroque, but Flemish rather than French.

The pomposity of the burghers of Ghent is reflected in their city palaces and country retreats. The rich spent the winter months in the city and retired to the country for the summer. Virtually every beech copse in the surroundings of Ghent hides a fine country home of classical design. Most of these retreats are still owned by the descendants of the original families. On those rare occasions when one of these houses comes on the market bidding is fierce.

The Hôtel d'Hane-Steenhuyse in Veldstraat is a superb example of a city mansion, even though it was built on a site which is far too narrow for this sublime house. The classical rear façade is well-bal   d, but the Baroque front is an inelegant mass of ʌone, fortunately not very conspicuous in the narrow street. The interior, on the other hand, is typically French and highly sophisticated. Chateaubriand tells us that Louis XVIII, the unfortunate French king, enjoyed his stay here tremendously. The king spent more than a hundred days in Ghent, being fêted by the local aristocracy who wined and dined him, serving him delicious meals in their best silverware. Some Ghent families still cherish the memory of this royal visit and have religiously kept the silverware used for the dishes they prepared for the king. During his stay in this small palace King Louis is certain to have listened to string quartets playing in the huge ballroom, more than two stories high and full of mirrors, with its Paris floor and its richly decorated ceiling.

When the citizens of Ghent wanted their homes decorated they could always appeal to the van Reysschoot family, a dynasty of painters who preferred the later Rubens to the less exuberant style of Poussin. They were clearly impressed by Watteau's *fêtes galantes*. Their light-hearted murals with dancing couples and hovering nude *putti* were immensely popular. Anyone who could afford it – and many could – commissioned one of the van Reysschoots to decorate their drawing rooms. Opulent murals, hidden underneath a coat of paint, are frequently rediscovered today in modest homes. Apparently, many ordinary tradesmen sought to emulate the rich. How delightful if you should find such a treasure in your own home !

It is not really surprising that murals abound in Flemish homes. The Flemish have always suffered from *horror vacui*, or the fear of empty spaces. Sadly, they seem to have finally got rid of their fear in the course of this century. But even in the time of the Flemish Primitives every single surface was covered with paint or sculpture, which created richly decorated interiors.

Whereas cities like Ghent flirted with the French, Antwerp looked to our Austrian rulers, as a walk along Meir will immediately show. This beautiful street boasts the heritage of a famous architect with a resounding name – Jan Pieter van Baurscheit the Younger. Of German descent, he had designed many houses for the patricians of Holland and Zeeland. One of them was Daniel Marot, the French huguenot who had settled in the Dutch United Provinces. Van Baurscheit built two portly mansions on Meir. The first, later to become a royal palace, is very impressive

Like many other Ghent mansions the Hôtel d'Hane-Steenhuyse was abundantly decorated with murals and frescoes. Underneath this flamboyant ceiling (left) the French King enjoyed his dinners.

Every door of this house has been provided with a supraporta in colour or grisaille. This playful cherub (left) can be found above one of the doors of the ballroom. At the time paintings in shades of grey were popular throughout Europe. Pieter Norbert van Reysschoot was one of the masters of the genre, as was the renowned Dutch artist Jacob de Wit.
Drawing rooms and parlours were lavishly decorated with wood carvings and oil paintings. In the Ghent area most commissions went to the van Reysschoot family.

The Hôtel d'Hane-Steenhuyse (left) in Veldstraat in Ghent is no doubt one of the most imposing mansions of the Low Countries. The three-storey high ballroom was decorated with large trompe l'oeils by Pieter Norbert van Reysschoot. Paris craftsmen took four years, from 1776 to 1780, to finish the parquetry floor. Weekly redoutes were held in this sumptuous decor, in honour of the exiled King Louis XVIII of France.

Leopold Mozart thought Ghent a dreary, modern city. And modern it was. It was also thoroughly French. The libraries were stacked with books by Voltaire, Rousseau and Saint-Simon. Actors from Paris regularly performed plays by Beaumarchais and Molière. Ghent was a fashionable city. The local architects devoutly studied the works of Jean Marot, Jacques-François Blondel and Germain Boffrand. Some houses would not have been out of place in the heart of Paris.

The Hôtel Falligan (right) in particular is decidedly French in inspiration, with its marble fireplaces à la royale, *its many light pastel hues and its exuberant rocailles. The best way to enjoy this interior is by candlelight, when the decorations cast dancing shadows (left).*

indeed; looking at its façade, you can easily imagine yourself to be in Vienna rather than in Antwerp. A short distance away is the flamboyant Osterrieth House, like its counterpart designed by van Baurscheit for the wealthy van Susteren family. It was built in Flemish Rococo style, with subtly carved rocailles over the windows and doors. These two showpieces established van Baurscheit's ascendancy over the other Antwerp architects. In the sixteenth and seventeenth centuries Italian and Spanish fashions had dominated Antwerp, but now inspiration came from the east.

Then came the nineteenth century, the epitome of architectural confusion, when architects in Antwerp and Brussels began to repeat the various styles of the past.

OPPOSITE ST. LUKE'S COLLEGE in Ghent, where generations of architects have studied, stands a mansion with a decaying façade. The building is large but not very conspicuous because it lacks ornamentation. Its present unadorned exterior dates from the end of last century, but the house itself is still in its original state. It seems like an island in the middle of the city, since its surroundings have been completely transformed, creating the impression that it has changed its location. Just over a century ago it was situated on a quay along Oude Houtlei, a narrow medieval canal running into the River Leie. At that time its façade would have been reflected in the water of the canal and wooden merchant ships would have anchored in front of it. This area used to be as picturesque as the most idyllic spot in Bruges. It is a pity that so many of Ghent's canals have been filled in. Fortunately, this house was preserved. It was designed by David 't Kindt, one of Ghent's most renowned architects, who was inspired by the work of Jacques François Blondel, the famous French architect. Building began in 1768. The politician Arthur Verhaegen used to live here, and his family still own the house, cherishing it with loving care. I know few town houses with such an abundance of atmosphere, something which no visitor can fail to notice. The entrance hall with its shining marble floor is infused with a peculiar kind of light, creating a quiet, melancholy mood. Perhaps this light is caused by the old glass in the windows or by the reflection of the rays of the sun on the stuccoed walls and ceiling. The unusual layout of the building strikes the visitor at once. All the rooms give out on a central hall; separate passages, a feature of nineteenth-century buildings, are noticeably absent. In eighteenth-century houses people had to cross from room to room. The rooms are built in a row and are connected by doors leading to the garden. This enfilade

design was seen as an aesthetic ideal. It has created a fine vista, running the length of the entire building. Adjacent to the street we find the Chinese room, where Chinese wallpaper, painted with cranes, pheasants, peacocks and partridges, creates an exotic atmosphere. This expensive wallpaper was pasted onto a linen frame. Originally the room may have been full of lacquered furniture, chinaware and other Oriental bric-a-brac. It is by no means the only Chinese room in the city. Many rooms in Ghent town houses and country retreats are furnished with this type of wallpaper, which was sometimes mounted on a silk frame, as in the Hôtel

Clemmen. The burghers of Ghent were obviously fond of *chinoiseries*. Oriental wallpaper was particularly popular in the eighteenth and early nineteenth centuries. The art historian Nicole De Bisscop has made a thorough study of these furnishings, discovering a link with the Ostend Company, which from 1723 onwards controlled the Flemish trade in Chinese luxury goods. For some time it was a major rival of the renowned Dutch East India Company. Many rich Ghent families were represented on the board of the Ostend Company. It seems likely that the wallpaper was brought back by their ships' captains.

This enfilade connects the sitting room with the dining room (left). Adjacent to the street is the Chinese room. The Hôtel Verhaegen once had two rooms hung with Chinese wallpaper (above). The citizens of Ghent were exceptionally fond of chinoiseries. The Chinese wallpaper was imported by the Ostend Company, a rival of the Dutch East India Company.

The dining room adjacent to the garden has a Baroque character because of its wealth of colour. Pieter Norbert van Reysschoot, the most important member of this family of painters, decorated it with five large panels and three *supraportas*. The panels portray fishermen, peasants and many shepherds in the evening twilight. Elegantly dressed citizens walk by on a wharf. One group in particular catches the eye, for it includes a man sitting on a bale of goods displaying the painter's initials. He is talking to a soldier, and one of the people standing near him seems Chinese. This pastoral scene hints at so many stories that it is impossible ever to become bored by it.

Finally there is the French-style garden with symmetric parterres of box hedges. The most beautiful item here is no doubt the sunny façade of the coachhouse, which at one time hid a separate world of servants' rooms, stables and even a private chapel. In this Rococo decor the owner must have felt as happy as a king.

The drawing room (left) of the Hôtel Verhaegen seems to bathe in a mellow light, softened by the drapes and the warm colours. Although the furniture was occasionally renewed during the past century, the atmosphere and the layout of this room have hardly changed.
Behind the Hôtel Verhaegen is a delightful garden where Mozart would have been happy to join us for a cup of tea. He would have felt at home here, for the sunny façades (left) recall his native country. The delicate colours of the coach house and the flamboyant dormer window are clear evidence that Flanders was once part of the Austrian Netherlands.

THERE IS JUST one place in Ypres where the atmosphere of Versailles is still alive and where you can imagine yourself to be in the company of Rousseau and Voltaire, discussing the merits of *fantaisie* and *raison*. This is the Hôtel Merghelynck, an eighteenth-century mansion, now a museum. You would hardly expect to find a house like this in a town where every single thing reminds you of the Great War. The Hôtel is a relic from the past, when Ypres was still dominated by Lille and French rather than Flemish was spoken here.

When the coach gate slams shut behind me, I seem to have entered a different world, returning to the Age of Enlightenment. The huge gate separates the house from the world outside and emphasizes the power of its occupants. You would hardly dare to cross the hall and catch a glimpse of the interior. Such familiarity would be frowned upon – you will have to wait until a servant has announced your arrival to the master of the house.

Once that has been done, you are allowed to enter the *boudoir de madame*, resembling a candy box filled with fine furniture and china ornaments. Here Madame Amélie Strabant, François-Ignace Merghelynck's wife, would sit down at her *bonheur du jour* to write letters to her friends, I assume, for there is still a goose quill on the desk, as well as a beautiful inkwell and some sheets of paper. It is as if you are in an apartment in Paris. To Madame Strabant France was, of course, the centre of the world. Ypres is only a few miles distant from Lille, where Thomas Gombert worked, the architect who designed this house. François Merghelynck himself liked to withdraw with his friends to the *chambre jaune*, a magnificent dining room in the masculine Louis-seize style. In this sumptuous decor he could lord it over his guests and dominate the conversation. During mealtimes the ideas of the Enlightenment were no doubt discussed. Entertain-ment was provided in the snug decor of the adjacent reception rooms. In the music room the honourable guests could listen to a string quartet while enjoying a cup of tea or cocoa. The immense wealth displayed in this house makes it eminently clear that the ladies and gentlemen gathered here had their own private inter-pretation of the concepts of *liberté, fraternité* and *égalité*, so dear to the Enlightenment. These subtle contradic-tions are also manifest in the decorations. Apart from the portraits of militant Roman-Catholic bishops there is also a bust of Voltaire. The French *façon de vivre* adopted by the people who lived here encouraged a light-hearted view of life. Even the colour scheme of the interior shows that the occupants of this house were *nouveaux riches*, for the colours are indicative of a subtle class struggle. 'Poor' colours, such as angel red, were taboo. Blue, too, was hardly used. When this house was completed in 1775 blue was no longer a symbol of wealth, as it had been before, when costly blue dyes were still made from ground lapis lazuli. When in 1724 the recipe for cheaper Berlin blue became known, the colour became so popular in simple homes that rich people stopped using it. That is why the architect of this house preferred a fashionable green for many rooms.

François Merghelynck and his wife lived mainly on the first floor, where they each had their own apart-ment, separated by a small dining room. Everything has been fully preserved. Madame Strabant lived at the back. Her bedroom has a view of the courtyard, a strategic location allowing her to watch over everything that went on in the house. Her bedroom also served as a *chambre de parade*, where she could receive close friends. She slept in her *lit à la Polonaise*, a doll-like little bed with a canopy, hidden away in a niche. The rooms fronting the street form a magnificent enfilade. They are opulently furnished with side-tables, easy chairs and cabinets displaying china bibelots. Precious oil paint-

Visitors are free to go where they like in the Hôtel Merghelynck, from the kitchen to Madame Amélie Strabant's room (left). Fortunately, she is no longer here to tell us off, as she would certainly have done, for only her closest friends were received in this room. They would have a cup of cocoa while Madame Strabant rested in her lit à la Polonaise. *The cocoa was poured from beautiful silver jugs, made by one of Ypres' highly talented silversmiths. If you are in luck, you may get a look at François-Ignace Merghelynck's wardrobe. His expensive coats of embroidered silk are still there. When the ladies went to the* appartement de madame *the gentlemen would accompany monsieur to the smoking room (right). First they would smoke a pipe and then play cards.*

Because the house was turned into a museum long ago, it was never renovated afterwards. That is why so much has been preserved, including even the chinaware the family used for summer picnics (right).
The house was actually built twice. At the end of last century it was saved from decay by a great-grandson of the original owner and furnished with antique furniture. But shortly after the outbreak of World War I Ypres, then one of the most beautiful medieval towns of Europe, was utterly destroyed. All that was left of the Hôtel Merghelynck was a part of the façade. Fortunately, all art treasures could be saved in time; they were exhibited in the Petit Palais in Paris for the duration of the war. After the war the building was expertly reconstructed.

ings hide the naughty fables by Jean de La Fontaine adorning the *Toile de Jouy*. In candlelight the stucco decorations in these small rooms change into marvellous monochromes.

The master of the house had his rooms on the street corner. His smoking room was painted brown, around 1775 the most fashionable colour in Paris. It was often contemptuously referred to as *merde d'oie* or *caca-dauphin*. Next to the smoking room is his bedroom, with in a corner by the bed the *cabinet d'aisance à soupape*.

The reddish-pink wall paintings shine in the generous sunlight. The small door next to the niche with the bed provides access to François Merghelynck's wardrobe. His summer suits and formal costumes are still hanging in this ancient cupboard as if they have not been touched for more than two centuries.

At the end of last century the Hôtel was saved from decay by Arthur Merghelynck, a great-grandson of the original owner. He bought it and had it furnished with antique furniture. But his life's work was destroyed by the war when virtually the entire town of Ypres was razed to the ground in 1915. Fortunately, the violence of war was not unexpected, so that all the art objects could be removed in time. During the remainder of the war the collection was shown in the Petit Palais in Paris. After the war the building, whose façade had been preserved, was expertly restored, with so much skill and subtlety that visitors feel as if they are in an authentic eighteenth-century house. Today, the Hôtel Merghelynck is a French island in Flanders.

One of the main attractions of the Hôtel Merghelynck is its rich variety of colours. Nowhere else does the eighteenth century look quite as cheerful and lively as it does here. Don't think, however, that it was all just improvisation. The colour scheme is evidence of an eighteenth-century class struggle. 'Poor' colours such as blue were hardly used, despite its popularity at the time. But the aristocracy preferred other colours, because blue was the colour of ordinary people. When it was still made of ground lapis lazuli it had been very expensive, but once the cheaper Berlin blue became available in 1724 the rich stopped using it.

Every room in this house has been given a different colour, ranging from red and brown to green and yellow. The chambre jaune was the magnificent dining room of Monsieur Merghelynck.

CASTLES AND STATELY HOMES

———

Flanders has few large moated castles, even though medieval castles are plentiful. Many feudal strongholds were transformed into stately homes and country retreats. Tillegem Castle (above) has escaped this fate.
Rumbeke Castle (right) used to be surrounded by water. With the partition of the Low Countries it lost its military use. It was renovated, but never rebuilt. Antiques dealer Eric Loncke has restored it to its former glory.

CASTLES SHOW WHAT landscapes were like. When stone or rock was not available, the knights of yore had to rely on water and swamps for their defence; they would construct earthen walls and build palisades. Many fortifications along the River Scheldt, which in the ninth century formed the frontier between Western Francia and the German Empire, were built in this way. Some of these bulwarks were lost, such as Ename near Oudenaarde, but others grew into cities like Ghent and Antwerp.

Donjons and fortified houses sprang up everywhere, built by local barons wanting to protect their possessions. Every village had a tower and a moat. Those fortifications that were later converted into country mansions have been preserved. Large castles are rare in Flanders. Some of these old buildings have kept their feudal character, for instance Cleydael Castle near Aartselaar, a brick moated castle with elegant turrets. Like Bossenstein, north of Lier, it was part of a ring of outposts defending Antwerp. Bossenstein is a small, impressive fortification dominated by an immense tower. Vorselaar Castle near Turnhout is one of the most imposing castles of Flanders. Like Tillegem Castle near Bruges it was adorned with battlements, embrasures and watchtowers at the height of Romanticism in the nineteenth century.

Following the many exhausting wars with Holland peace finally returned to Flanders in the seventeenth century. The castles were turned into stately homes for the aristocracy. The battlements were removed from the watchtowers and the façades elegantly decorated. The picturesque fairy-tale castle of Rumbeke is an excellent example. It was restored to its former glory by Eric Loncke, an antiques dealer. Ooidonk Castle, built on a bend in the River Leie during the Middle Ages, is another fortification that lost its use as an observation post in the seventeenth century. It was later rebuilt in Flemish Renaissance style.

In the eighteenth century many rich citizens had their own country retreats. Fortified farmhouses were turned into mansions in the French style. The area around Ghent in particular teems with stately homes and ornate gardens. French influence shows in the use of mansard roofs and luxuriantly stuccoed interiors. Leeuwergem Castle with its huge pond and open-air theatre is perhaps the best representative of this style. There was an enormous variety of styles and designs. Heks Castle near Tongeren, for instance, is a fine example of Liège Rococo.

Later architects tried to emulate the great Italian masters. The Neo-Classical stately home of Wannegem-Lede is often compared to the Petit Trianon in Versailles. The interior has been flamboyantly decorated with stucco designs by Moretti, the Italian designer. It has a delightful Chinese room – Alphonse Baut de Rasmont, its original owner, was a director of the Ostend Company.

In the nineteenth century historicism led to an indiscriminate revival of earlier styles. Flemish architects took their inspiration from their great English counterparts. The first designs of Loppem Castle were in fact made by Augustus Pugin, the renowned London architect. Bornem Castle, built by Hendrik Beyaert in 1888, looks as if it is part of the set of an opera. It seems to have been inspired by Neuschwanstein, the fake medieval castle of Louis II, the flamboyant Bavarian king.

AXEL VERVOORDT, an antiques dealer, lives 'between dream and reality' in a moated castle, set in a huge park with romantic outbuildings and an orangery. 's Gravenwezel Castle is a green oasis on the edge of the village. It is hidden from view by a circle of oak woods. The trees have been there for more than two centuries, something which fascinates Vervoordt, because vegetation is the most vulnerable part of a landscape. Avenues which are hundreds of years old are irreplaceable. Besides, Vervoordt says, trees will considerably improve an ugly landscape. His many travels have convinced him of the close link between the preservation of historical buildings and the conservation of nature. Verwoordt favours subtle restorations, feeling that changes should be kept to a minimum. His own home bears this out. Even the peeling castle walls have not been repainted. Visitors used to be critical of his approach, but gradually they have come to understand that an age-old patina helps to merge a building with its natural environment. The plants covering the walls have become one with the flaking and decaying façades that blend imperceptibly with the surrounding woods. Achieving a harmonious ensemble is what really matters, Vervoordt argues. He attaches great importance to the correct proportions of objects and buildings. Craftsmen used to have a better eye for proportions than they do now, he says, referring to nineteenth-century houses to support this view. Even small, simple houses would be built according to a nicely balanced plan. Craftsmen, using only a knotted rope for measurements, would always manage to get the proportions right. Every part of such houses, from plinths to windows, would be perfectly balanced.

It has taken Vervoordt years to fully understand the principles of this type of harmony. The results are visible in his castle, where decoration has been elevated to an art form. Vervoordt doesn't bother with conventional ideas about matching styles and periods. He does not hesitate to combine a Lucio Fontana painting with a seventeenth-century Antwerp cabinet. He refuses to be restricted by such simplistic concepts as 'antique' or 'modern' and is fascinated by anything that is timeless. His interest is not limited to old things but extends equally to contemporary art. Unlike many other collectors Vervoordt doesn't buy antiques in order to travel back to the past.

's Gravenwezel Castle is just a stone's throw from the hectic port of Antwerp, and it is a relief to spend some time here, away from the city. Two centuries ago it was rebuilt for just this purpose, when it became the country home of an Antwerp family, the van Susterens. Anyone approaching the building along the driveway would hardly suspect to find a beautiful mansion at the end of it, because the north-facing part of the building is completely different from the part facing south. The southern façade is that of an elegant summer residence; the northern façade belongs to a sturdy medieval castle with a moat and massive turrets.

Jan Alexander van Susteren had the castle rebuilt in 1740 by the celebrated Austrian architect Jan Pieter van Baurscheit the Younger to bring it into line with the new fashions. The high walls were pulled down and the drawbridge was removed, to be replaced by a large terrace with a view of the open country. It is now the favourite spot for Axel Vervoordt and his family to have breakfast. An elegant façade, crowned with a large pediment, was added to the south terrace. Van Baurscheit also modernized the outbuildings.

Isn't it wonderful that a namesake of the present owner, the sculptor Michiel Vervoort the Elder, collaborated with van Baurscheit ? Together with Artus Quellinus the Younger he was the most important eighteenth-century Flemish sculptor. Michiel Vervoort made the garden statues, which have unfor-

tunately been lost. The castle was badly in need of repair when Axel Vervoordt bought it. His painstaking restoration was a veritable voyage of discovery, because so many traces from the past were brought to light. Much care has been given to an authentic recreation of the building's history. The garden and the rooms facing it radiate the optimism of the eighteenth century. The focus of attention in this part of the castle is Axel Vervoordt's study. The antique marquetry floor, dividing the room into snug little compartments, is a gem. The Chippendale bookcases and the Empire wallpaper create a distinguished atmosphere. But this room is a place for work and not for rest. If you want to relax you should go to the library, the building's beating heart, where the Vervoordts withdraw in the evening and during the winter. The library also houses a curio collection with many precious objects ranged among the books.

The northern part of the castle takes you back to the past. The music room, for instance, set behind the study, recalls the Age of Humanism with its Renaissance interior. To someone from Antwerp like Vervoordt the Renaissance was, of course, a Golden Age to be fondly remembered. After all, in the sixteenth century Antwerp was the world's most important centre of the art trade. Families like the Forchondts and the Mussons had agents throughout the known world, from Paris to Lisbon. They exported all kinds of luxury goods, including tapestries, silverware, jewellery, mirrors, paintings and musical instruments. The harpsichords fashioned by the Antwerp instrument makers Hans and Andreas Ruckers, for instance, were in great demand. It was an era when arts and crafts flourished throughout Flanders. Most of the resulting products were shipped to the rest of the world by way of Antwerp. It would not be amiss to compare Axel Vervoordt to one of these Renaissance art dealers,

Antiques dealer Axel Vervoordt has subtly restored the castle and decorated it with beautiful antiques. His office-cum-library has a magnificent parquetry floor (left). This is where he receives guests. The room has witnessed many conversations, but they have not always been about antiques. Vervoordt rejects simple notions like 'antique' and 'modern'. Contemporary art he finds fascinating as well. Unlike many other collectors he does not buy antiques in an attempt to travel back to the past. That is why he is not afraid to set off a Chinese Ming vase with a painting by Lucio Fontana.

since he works for an international clientele as well.

His castle, however, is not like a museum at all. It is a place to live in, because Vervoordt has created an ensemble, a single work of art. All elements fit together and everyone, from the restorer to the craftsman repairing old locks, feels at home here.

's Gravenwezel Castle was completely refurnished by antiques dealer Axel Vervoordt. The dining room (left), containing beautiful Ming china, is reminiscent of a Bohemian interior with its light colours, its Baroque mirror, its abundant sunlight and its summery furniture. Jan Alexander van Susteren, the castle's original owner, and Jan Peter van Baurscheit the Younger, its renowned Austrian architect, would doubtless have felt at home in this room.

Adjacent to the garden are fine outbuildings with stables and sheds, a pigeon house and an orangery. Here are also the picturesque workshops of the restorers, blacksmiths and cabinetmakers. This is the small smithy, where locks and keys are made or repaired.

Beyond the kitchen, where most visitors do not go, we discovered this sublime vista (left). A single glance at the view is sufficient to make us understand the life-style of the castle's residents.
We also descended to the immense cellars of the castle (above). Here we find the old kitchen, which is still occasionally used for cooking, mostly when dinner parties are held. At such times the best dinnerware is used.

During his hundred days' stay in Ghent, the French King Louis XVIII commuted between the Hôtel d'Hane-Steenhuyse and Leeuwergem Castle (right). The castle, more than two hundred years old, is set on an island in the middle of a lake decorated with two sphinxes. The park, part of which is open to the public, is better known than the castle. One of its main attractions is the open-air theatre, made of trimmed hornbeam. The boxes seat an audience of more than a thousand. Occasionally operas are performed here.

DISCREETLY HIDDEN in the fold of a hill Leeuwergem Castle presents itself to the visitor. It used to be the country home of an aristocratic family, who came here to enjoy the peace and quiet of nature, away from the bustling city. Two centuries ago people apparently felt that need as much as we do.

This stately home stands at the end of a long avenue lined with age-old beeches separating the estate from the world outside. It is situated in one of Flanders' most charming parks, a mysterious pleasure ground full of surprises that gradually unfold themselves to the visitor. The open-air theatre is no doubt the principal landmark. This structure of trimmed hornbeam is quite unique. It is hidden from view by lofty beeches. These trees provide an ideal sound box for this large natural theatre which seats more than 1000 people. Plays and concerts are occasionally performed here, including a recent performance of Mozart's opera *Bastien and Bastienne*. At the far end of the park is a beech wood with small canals and several ponds. Various structures and memorials are set among the trees, including a copy of Jean-Jacques Rousseau's tomb, engraved with the words *Carpe Diem* in ornamental lettering. It seems an appropriate motto for this idyllic place.

The house itself is mirrored in a large pond, guarded by two sphinxes lying down. These fabled creatures have been in the same spot for almost two centuries. They were put here shortly after the castle was plundered by French revolutionaries. A hundred years later the castle became the property of the della Faille d'Huysse family. Baron Baudoin della Faille, the present owner, runs the estate with great care, refusing to turn his home into a museum. Occasional visitors are welcome, but the castle is primarily residential in character. The open-air theatre is open to the public, however, and the orangery has been restored.

The interior has been furnished with great dedication; the eighteenth century is present everywhere. The building differs visibly from the large castles of an earlier age. The rooms are not much larger than those of a town house. When the castle was built people were beginning to set more store by comfort. Pleasant boudoir furniture predominates in the snug interior. The layout of the building is rectangular, with a large central hall around which all the rooms have been grouped. The hall gives out on the *appartement de société*, where guests are received. At the time when the castle was built, in 1724, the era of grand society balls was past so that smaller, interlinked rooms were preferred, connected by folding doors. The most intimate rooms, decorated in Rococo style, are in the southern part of the building. The main room, which may have seen a lot of exuberant feasting, was added twenty-five years later. The decorations in this room are remarkably international. The mantelpiece is a fine design by Robert Adam, the Scottish architect. Adam was deeply impressed by the ruins of Pompey, which had then only just been discovered, and used them as his main source of inspiration. The room is hung with Chinese wallpaper portraying an exotic garden full of birds. It is an excellent place to enjoy a cup of tea or cocoa served in antique chinaware.

If the former residents were to return, they would be much surprised to see that the chapel with its delightful decorations has been preserved intact. Everything has remained as it was, including the stucco designs and the statuary. Even the skilfully marbled walls have been left untouched.

Leeuwergem Castle has rooms suitable for every moment of the day. This room with its view of the lake is a good place to be at noontime. Lucky visitors may see the rippling water being reflected on the ceiling and hear the ducks quacking outside. This is the quietest room of the castle.

Remove the altar and you are left with just an ordinary living room. The elegant stucco decorations create an atmosphere of intimacy and comfort. This has always been Leeuwergem Castle's private chapel. It is discreetly hidden in a corner on the building's first floor. Miraculously, the chapel has remained intact. Rooms like these were frequently redecorated and the walls remarbled. But it is obvious

that these walls have been left untouched for more than two hundred years.

From the air Marke Castle near Kortrijk (above) looks like a golden pinpoint in a green park. This oasis is situated among busy traffic arteries and was lucky to escape being bombed during World War II. The de Béthune family, who use the castle as a summer residence, take loving care of it. A few years ago it was repainted, not quite the routine job you may think it is, because colour schemes are an essential element of this type of architecture. When the interior was redecorated the family travelled to Vicenza to study the colours used by Palladio. The original colours of the interior, hidden under a thick layer of grey paint, also helped in deciding what colour scheme to use.

MARKE CASTLE, a sun-temple on a green island near Kortrijk, has miraculously escaped the frenzied building activities of our time. Some years ago its façades were repainted in the original colours. The magnificent colour schemes with their pink and yellow hues emphasize the distinctive architecture of this stately home, built from 1802 to 1805 in a style linking Empire and Directoire. Art historians used to be somewhat disparaging of this period, which, however, has come back into favour since the recent bicentenary celebration of the French Revolution.

Baron Emmanuel de Béthune, who uses the castle as a summer residence, has always been aware of the special charm of his country retreat. Some years ago he began to restore the building, a fragile work of art made of simple materials like brick, mortar and wood. Since the sumptuous decor simply consists of stucco and paint renovation had to be carried out with much caution. The first step was to check old records to find out about the original decorations. At the end of last century every room in the house had been repainted in a dull *gris Trianon*, the colour of the Trianon pavilion in Versailles. People used to think that grey was a typical eighteenth-century colour, but this turned out to be quite untrue. After the de Béthune family had spent many weekends clearing away old coats of paint the original, surprising colours of the house reemerged. The dining room presents a colourful whole, rich in delicate *faux marbre* with unusual hues. The interior was carefully redecorated in oil paints. The expert restoration of the colour scheme has re established the link with the original source of inspiration. The architects, Pisson from Ghent and Dewarlez from Lille, had borrowed their designs from Andrea Palladio, the celebrated Renaissance architect. Baron de Béthune and his family travelled to Vicenza to study Palladian villas and did in fact discover there all the types of marbling displayed in the interior of their own home.

It is no wonder that the family are so fond of this house, as it was built by Baron de Béthune's great-great-grandfather. No fewer than eight generations have lived under its roof. They all spent the first months of their lives in the same beautiful mahogany cradle, which the Emperor Napoleon once received as a present from the city of Bordeaux.

When Marke Castle was built, Flanders was prospering. At that time the region was part of France, so that Flemish cloth manufacturers were allowed to export their goods throughout the French Empire. Many families grew rich. By 1830 a large number of these manufacturers had become landowners or had entered politics. Most of the country homes they built in the Scheldt valley between Kortrijk and Ghent were rebuilt and adapted to new fashions by later generations. Only a few have been preserved in their original state. Marke Castle itself narrowly escaped a similar fate. Jean de Béthune, the founder of the Gothic revival in Flanders and the grandfather of the present occupier, spent four consecutive summers here. If he should have stayed longer, he would no doubt have converted the building into a medieval abode. He did in fact remove the ornamental caryatids from the dining room because they seemed too profane and replaced them with flowers. Fortunately they were stored in the attic and later put back.

Marke Castle was built in the early years of last century, when Flanders was under French rule. The union with France meant that Flemish cloth manufacturers could sell their products on a huge market. Many families grew rich, especially in the Kortrijk area.

Near Kortrijk they built splendid Empire-style summer residences. Marke Castle, however, displays elements of the Directoire period as well. Its two architects, Pisson from Ghent and Dewarlez from Lille, inevitably borrowed from the great Paris masters. This exuberant stairway betrays the influence of the French architects Percier and Fontaine.

Fortunately, this castle has survived
the Gothic revival. It was a narrow
escape, as the originator of the
Flemish Neo-Gothic movement,
Jean de Béthune, lived here for a
while. He could easily have
transformed it into a medieval
stronghold.
Most of the original furniture has
been preserved, including some
mahogany Empire furniture from
Zeeland. Instead of bronze
mountings painted wood was used,
as bronze was scarce.

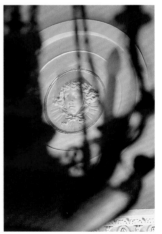

The valleys of the Rivers Leie and Scheldt cut Flanders in two. For many centuries these rivers were of great strategic importance, so that medieval strongholds abound in the region between Ghent, Oudenaarde, Kortrijk and Tournai. Many of them were pulled down, but some were transformed into summer residences. Located on riverbanks or on sloping ground they were ideally suited for this purpose. Ooidonk Castle was imaginatively restored and refurnished in the nineteenth century. Its drawing rooms are exceptionally beautiful. The owners cherish their castle and have decorated it with Flemish Renaissance art, including tapestries and cabinets.

I T IS DIFFICULT to imagine that a majestic building like Ooidonk Castle was actually built in the middle of a swamp. Its strategic location in the valley of the River Leie meant that it was repeatedly besieged and plundered. In 1579 the Calvinists finally destroyed it. Half a century later it was rebuilt in a severe Flemish Renaissance style. The swamp has long gone. It has been magically transformed into fields, oak woods, long avenues lined with lime trees and beautiful French gardens. The interior of the castle is like a passage through time. But the Renaissance dominates with many Flemish tapestries and Antwerp cabinets.

Loppem Castle (right) is no doubt the finest Neo-Gothic building in Flanders. It is also one of the oldest examples of the Gothic revival, having been built from 1858 to 1863. Its austere façades betray English influence. The castle's Neo-Gothic style reflects the religious beliefs of its original owner, Baron Charles van Caloen. Unlike Neo-Renaissance or Neo-Classicism, which were rejected as being pagan, Neo-Gothic architecture was supposed to be Christian in inspiration. From 1900 onwards Belgium came under the spell of Art Nouveau and Functionalism. These styles spread so rapidly that Neo-Gothic architecture soon became unfashionable. Fortunately, much has been preserved. Loppem Castle is in excellent condition, thanks to the efforts of the van Caloen family. The interior is fully intact. The castle contributes to a reappraisal of Neo-Gothic architecture. Now that the Gothic revival has become the subject of thorough study, we begin to realize how important this movement has been.

L OPPEM CASTLE seems to have been taken straight from the pages of a novel by Sir Walter Scott. Edward Pugin, its architect, a son of Augustus Pugin, who built the Houses of Parliament in Westminster, was clearly inspired by the age of chivalry. The castle was completed by Baron Jean de Béthune, who also designed all the details of the interior. The entrance hall even contains a Gothic billiard table. The original furnishings, including murals and furniture, have been fully preserved. The cluttered interior is typical for the nineteenth century, but it is impressive nevertheless. The van Caloen family, the original owners, chose a Neo-Gothic style because this was supposed to be a Christian type of architecture, unlike Neo-Renaissance or Classicism, which were associated with paganism. The building, which is open to the public, has been expertly restored by the family. The art collection includes many medieval objects and paintings.

THE COUNTRYSIDE
—

The Flemish countryside changes every ten to fifteen miles. Each region has its own distinctive character. The polders are full of gnarled willows eagerly drawing water from the soil. Here and there you can see clumps of reeds lining stretches of water where geese from the North alight in winter. This land was reclaimed from the sea. The earliest reclamation work was undertaken in the Middle Ages by religious communities, which derived considerable benefits from the new polders. It was a long time before the area had been fully drained. In the Westhoek, the region beyond the River Yser, water kept rising to the marshy surface. These marshes (right), known as the Moeren, were finally drained only a few centuries ago.

THE FLEMISH COAST is never more beautiful than when rain is pouring down and tumbling clouds break like waves over the country. At such times you feel that this country truly belongs to the sea. You can smell it in the salty air. When you go for a walk in the empty Booitshoeke polders near Veurne you can see distant green shapes gradually emerging on the horizon. They are dunes, a narrow ridge of sand vulnerable to the lightest breeze and often partially destroyed by storms. And yet they have been there for thousands of years and have been inhabited for almost as long. The first settlers were saltmakers and fishermen. The salt was originally traded by the Celtic lords living on the Kemmelberg; later it was used by the Romans. The Kemmelberg is situated near Poperinge, a good distance away from the coast. This 'mountain' is barely 515 feet high – a molehill rather than a true mountain. Dominating a flat landscape that hardly rises above sea level, it offers a distant view into France. That is why the Celts built a powerful hill fort on top of it.

The dunes protect the polders against the fury of the sea. In this flat country with its large fields and broad willow-lined ditches many buildings are nearly as old as the land itself. They have brick walls, made of locally found clay. Huge brick churches soar up in this thinly

populated area. The people who built them must have assumed that every village would grow into a town, but their hopes were defeated. City people do not feel at home in this farming region.

Country estates are rare in the polders along the coast and the Scheldt valley. The rich used to prefer the regions farther inland, settling in the hills of south-west Flanders. This rolling country is part of a long range of hills running from Cape Gris-Nez in France to the Ronse region, Pajottenland and Haspengouw. Thousands of years ago they formed an erratic coastline; at that time the areas around Antwerp, Bruges and Ghent were still covered by the sea. With its patchwork of fields and meadows, this is a very picturesque region. Many fresh-water springs are found here, contributing to the excellent beers that are brewed in the area. Where water rose to the surface parks were laid out, ponds were dug and country homes built. The entire region, from the Zwalm District to Breugelland near Brussels and Leuven, is densely wooded and exceptionally fertile, as the many beautiful villages and huge farmhouses attest. The Haspengouw region is an extension of this area with its fertile loam-soil. Roman barrows and endless yellow wheatfields meet the eye everywhere. Fruit trees have been planted on virtually every slope, making this region the orchard of Flanders.

MONIQUE VAN SPRANG seems to have a thing for landscape painters without being aware of it. She grew up on an estate near Liège, in a hilly region much in demand by the local Impressionists. A quarter of a century ago she went to live in Deurle, a village on the banks of the River Leie, which together with Sint-Martens-Latem is the Flemish equivalent of Barbizon. Just as in this French village on the edge of the Forest of Fontainebleau, generations of artists have here immortalized the landscape on canvas. The Leie, meandering through the fields, provides this flat, marshy land with a heavenly light. That was exactly what Monique had been looking for. Her house is not situated along the river, but on slightly higher ground, on the edge of a wood. The tall trees around the house create an atmosphere of timelessness, filling you with a sense of awe for the passing of the seasons. Seen from outside it is a modest home. The oldest part dates from more than two centuries ago. It was once used as an inn and a post office. Unfortunately, the Swedish artist who lived here in the fifties destroyed the house. The decorations disappeared and only the walls were left standing. Monique has taken that shapeless mass of stone and modelled it into a charming house where she exhibits her huge collection of curios.

True collectors of antiques and bric-a-brac are explorers of the past, she says. They go in search of things that nobody is interested in. Consequently, her collection includes many objects that people would simply throw away. If she had not got hold of the old-fashioned pharmacy cabinet that is now being used as a bookcase in the living room, it would have gone up in flames. Long ago, before everybody started collecting antiques, secondhand furniture was often cut up and used as kindling. This was something Monique van Sprang could not accept.

Her activities as a collector took her to many European countries, even as far as southern Italy. She had no trouble in finding objects of interest, as there was still a large supply. But getting her finds transported was something else again. As she did not have a van, she used to load everything in her deux-chevaux. In this way a huge baking grid from a Provençal bakery arrived in Deurle. Now this trophy graces her kitchen. Without her knowing it she even achieved local fame in Saint-Tropez. A friend of hers, who lived there, had also begun collecting things. As she had been inspired by Monique she called her finds 'sprangeries'.

This neologism apparently found favour with secondhand dealers in Saint Tropez. One day Monique entered an antiques shop and was asked what 'sprangeries' she was looking for! The shopkeeper had trouble, of course, pronouncing the foreign word and Monique could hardly believe her ears.

Her love of antiques goes back to her childhood, when she grew up among many beautiful heirlooms. First she collected old toys. Her interest was awakened by a present from her father, who gave each of his children a home-made miniature merry-go-round. Soon this toy was joined by antique doll's houses and cardboard theatres.

Monique van Sprang does not like showy objects. She prefers bric-a-brac and utensils and is fond of shop furniture. In addition to the pharmacy cabinet and the baking grid she has a genuine chopping block from an old-fashioned butcher's. She uses it to display the fresh vegetables she buys at the market every day. Her kitchen is really an exhibition room, for it contains hundreds of showpieces. A tangle of wicker baskets, birdcages and copper kettles hangs from the ceiling. On shelves along the wall are old-fashioned kitchen utensils.

The bedrooms, too, show that she feels completely

Monique's passion for antiques dates from her childhood, when she was surrounded by beautiful things. The dining room (left) is reminiscent of the castle where she grew up. The china, silverware and old paintings create an atmosphere of grandeur befitting an aristocratic interior. Fortunately, her house is large enough for her to be able to store all her possessions. Monique does not like showy objects, but prefers more expressive bibelots. The living room is cluttered with small tables set with silver tobacco boxes, crystal decanters and chinaware. Hidden among the antique watches and snuff boxes is even a genuine chastity belt. The marble Rococo fireplace provides a French touch.

at home in the country. She has furnished these small rooms with cherry and mahogany furniture. Rooms like these are not mere bedrooms. They are places where you can relax and forget that the end of the twentieth century is approaching.

Collecting is in Monique van Sprang's blood. It was her father who set it all off. One day he gave all his daughters a home-made toy as a present. Monique got a beautiful miniature merry-go-round that actually worked and had lots of little lights that could be switched on and off. It must have taken him hours to make it. Eventually, this showpiece was joined by antique doll's houses and tiny cardboard theatres. Her collection is now proudly displayed in a bedroom (right). Of course, the merry-go-round has been given the place of honour in the centre of the display. After a while Monique began collecting other things in addition to antique dolls. When she started her collection several decades ago, it was really something of a rescue operation, because so many beautiful things were then simply thrown away.

This kitchen (above) seems like a painting by Johannes Vermeer or Pieter de Hooch, even though it belongs to a later age, for the decorated table top on the wall postdates the work of these artists by more than a century. But all the components are there, from the shining floor to the tall fireplace and the mysterious light. This interior is typically Flemish, even though some of the objects are French. Nowhere else can such baroque and picturesque kitchens be found. The flowers in the centre of the table (right), the delftware and the copper utensils simply cry out to be painted. It is a scene that evokes smells and sounds. You can hear the clatter of dishes being washed up and the bubbling noises of pots simmering on the fire. Of course, there is the smell of pies being baked and the mouth-watering aroma of fresh jam.

EVEN WITHOUT CATCHING a glimpse of the surrounding landscape, you notice at once that this is a rural home. It has escaped time. Whatever role fashion may have played here, it has never been decisive. None of the people who have lived here have ever tried to impose a single style on the house. It seems that rather than slavishly following the various architectural fashions of the past century and a half they have preferred to introduce piecemeal changes in the interior and furnishings. People living in the country are often less vainglorious than city dwellers. They are quite content with less comfort and display. Consequently, you will hardly find any gilt surfaces in this house. Instead, earthly colours such as ochre, umber and siena predominate, perhaps because the residents feel close to the farming community. Here and there even the old-fashioned wallpaper has been preserved. Most of the furniture was inherited; only a few pieces were bought from antiques dealers. Many ornaments were handed down from earlier generations.

Situated as it is in the south-west of Flanders near the French border, the house shows the influence of French culture. The kitchen, on the other hand, reminds you of Dutch interiors with its fine black-and-white tiles and Delft Blue on the mantelpiece. Similar houses can be found in Picardy and Hainaut. Their interiors tend to be similar as well, with much polished oak, shining crystal and Tournai china.

The back part of the house has a decidedly rural character – hardly surprising, because this is where the cattle-sheds used to be. There is still an old greenhouse where delicious blue grapes are grown. In a corner of the garden is an old cabin where riders used to hang their saddles. Now it houses old birdcages and wicker baskets that were collected from local farmers. Collecting such objects is really something of a rescue operation, since they are often simply thrown away.

The front part of the house is clearly reminiscent of city architecture. The drawing room, used to receive family and friends, had to show a certain degree of wealth. But even here the furnishings are not unduly opulent. Nor do they have to be, for the true wealth of this house is in its charm and its rural peace and quiet. My favourite spot is the small entresol room next to the kitchen. It is undeniably the most intimate part of the house, and it is a delight to spend some time there. Rooms like these are a characteristic feature of rural Flemish architecture. They used to be built over vaulted cellars where food was stored. Dry and hot, these rooms were ideal places for hanging sides of ham. Linen was kept in the built-in cupboards next to the fireplace. This particular room was also used as an office, for there is an elegant roll top desk set against one of the walls.

The central stairway is hidden away in a corner, evidence that the house was built without the help of an architect. The work was done two centuries ago by a contractor who did not even bother to use a groundplan. A labyrinth of passages and rooms was simply added to an existing house, and this is precisely what creates the charm of the present building.

The first floor contains the master bedroom with wallpaper dating from the early nineteenth century. The room is furnished with Biedermeier furniture. Biedermeier was a reaction to the austerity of the Empire style. Still, Napoleon feels at home here, for his bust is prominently displayed in the centre of the reading room. In this room the family history is kept behind the antique bubbled glass of the bookcases. It is the quietest room in the house.

This is the perfect marriage of town and country. The rooms where guests are received (left and above) breathe an atmosphere of urban geniality. Large chandeliers, mahogany furniture and several paintings go to create a stylish and dignified environment. But the entresol room (above) and the naively sculpted bust of Napoleon (right) belong in a rural abode.

Many Flemish owe their fortunes to wine and grapes. Wine was imported from France, at first by way of Bruges and later via Antwerp and Ostend. Claret in particular was in great demand. There were also some domestic wines; indeed, wine-making has recently seen something of a revival in Flanders. Grapes were grown everywhere. From the eighteenth century onwards each country home had an orangery where orange trees and laurels were protected against winter frosts. Usually there was room for grapevines as well.

This house, too, was provided with a greenhouse some two hundred years ago. It contains a huge grapevine producing delicious blue grapes.

The man who built this house was as eccentric as his creation itself. He was a manufacturer whose ideas were amazingly progressive for his time. This towering house with its peculiar glass oriel (below) is a medieval folly. It is set in a small park with tall trees soaring up above a Neo-Gothic privy. The garden was restored and planted with many low hedges. The house was listed for demolition, as no-one was interested in this oddity. It has now been restored so successfully that you would not be surprised if its original owner suddenly entered the living room (next page).

THIS IS NOT a house but a folly, built in a small park next to a factory in Temse. Jérome Orlay, the original owner, must have been fond of castles, for in 1881 he had this tall house built in medieval style. Orlay was clearly obsessed by Gothic architecture. Even the privy, resembling an arbour underneath an old oak tree, has pointed arches. Everywhere in the house are inscriptions with admonishing or edifying slogans to persuade visitors of Orlay's nobility of soul. Orlay was in fact a very humanitarian employer. The workers in his spinning mill benefited from a form of social security, which was highly unusual at the time. Orlay also provided them with a library where they could borrow uplifting literature. But they were not allowed to sing while at work, because he thought that their folksongs were immoral.

Miraculously, the house has been preserved in its original state. When the present owners bought it, it was in very bad repair and on the point of being pulled down because hardly anyone showed any interest in it. By now it has been fully restored and painstakingly renovated, with a minimum of change. It has been furnished in an appropriate style. Neo-Gothic furniture was chosen for the large drawing room, where guests are received in a medieval setting. The living room is on the first floor. Here Orlay preferred a more intimate style with a touch of Classicism. The sitting room and study were refurnished according to late nineteenth-century fashions. They offer a magnificent view of the garden, which has been divided into small compartments, mirroring the rooms of the house. The present owners are clearly proud of their home. When answering the phone they solemnly identify themselves by saying 'Hello, this is the Orlay residence'.

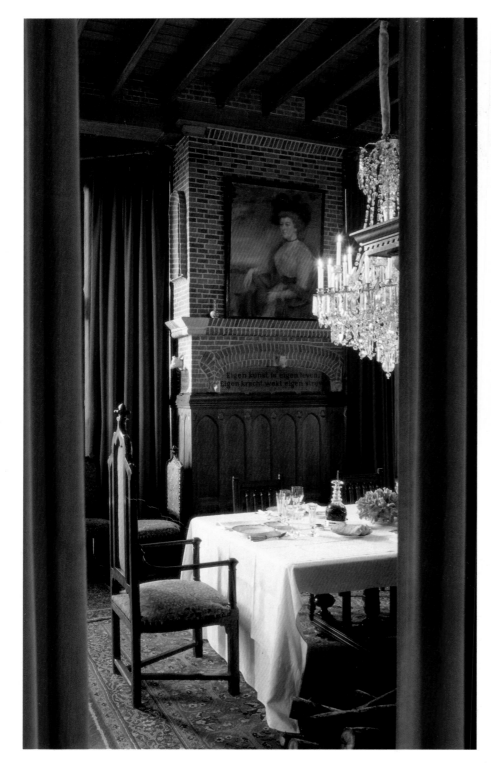

It seems likely that the interior was at least partly designed by the original owner himself. Wherever you look, you see slogans and aphorisms as well as sculptured heads. The interior is so fanciful that the house, despite its Gothic shape, does not have a medieval soul at all. It was furnished with a notable lack of rigidity. These are the dining room (left) and the study (above).

This is where the goat farm really comes to life (right). Here, in the warm kitchen, the young goats are reared before they are put in their sheds. As in the past, the animals are fed directly through the feeding hatches. The business was set up by an architect who never dreamed that she would once run a farm.

ARCHITECT AURÉLIE HERMANT never thought that one day she would run a farm. Her arrival here was a trick of fate. Having worked in her father's office in Paris for many years, she decided, after her father died, to visit Herckenrode Abbey near Hasselt, where as a child she had spent her holidays. She rediscovered the immense charm of this magnificent estate, once one of the largest abbeys in the Low Countries. When one of the many farmhouses on the estate came up for sale she decided to buy it, because she wanted at all costs to prevent it from becoming just another second home. She began reading books about breeding goats and making cheese and started a cheese farm. She bought her first goats through an advertisement in a newspaper. In just a few years she managed to turn the farm into a flourishing business producing exquisite cheeses. The farmhouse is a veritable monument because hardly anything has been changed. Even the feeding hatches between the kitchen and the sheds are still in use.

The house where Aurélie lives, a converted cattle-shed, is situated a small distance away on the estate, near the abbey itself. She has furnished it with pieces of abbey furniture that survived the French Revolution. The most beautiful item is a huge refectory table from the middle of the seventeenth century. Aurélie and her husband Bertrand Limbourg, a photographer, spend their lives here surrounded by history.

Until the French Revolution Herckenrode Abbey was one of the richest estates of the Low Countries. Since then the church has gone and the abbess's quarters have been restored in poor taste. Fortunately, the infirmary has been well preserved. It has a monumental stairway (above), once more betraying southern European influence. The cramp irons on the façade indicate that it was built in 1658. At that time the Reformation was in full swing and Flanders was ruled by the Spanish. This interior

may formerly have been even more opulent, for the whitewashed walls probably hide colourful murals.

Aurélie and Bertrand live in a converted shed among antiques from the abbey, such as the superb refectory table from 1645. The bookcase contains part of the archives, which are now being put in order by a historian. The linen cupboard is beautifully decorated with faux-bois. Its heavy, Baroque design betrays Westphalian influence and is a reminder that Germany is not far away. The sixteenth-century majolica tile was taken from the floor of the demolished church.

MULLEM IS JUST a dot on the map between Ghent and Oudenaarde. Surrounded by green, this picturesque village with its windmill nestles on the slope of a low hill. On a clear day you can see the towers of Ghent. On the top of the hill is an old beech wood and beyond it a small castle. A twisting cobbled road descends to the village square. Here you enter a world where everything is in harmony, thanks to the efforts of the baron who owns virtually the entire village. He sees to it that every house is covered with a coat of ochre plaster. The village used to be an important demesne, as its sturdy churchtower shows. In the sixteenth century Mullem was a praetorium, the residence of the commander of an army camp. Vincent Verlinden's house is situated where the courthouse used to be, with a pillory next to it. After the French Revolution the building was replaced by a house that at one time served as a pub and later as the burgomaster's office.

In Mullem Verlinden has rediscovered the peacefulness of the English countryside he loves so much. On a visit to the USA two years ago he got to know New England with its many wooden houses, which he came to adore and which served as a source of inspiration for the redecoration of his own home. Small details betray this American influence, such as the high plinths and the muted hues of the walls. What Verlinden admires in rural architecture are its simplicity and stylish proportions. Also, rural homes are always perfectly oriented. In Verlinden's own home sunlight penetrates every single room, creating a brilliant interaction with the objects in the interior. Verlinden is not interested in art treasures, but in objects that have an emotional impact on him. He likes utensils such as a pastrycook's earthenware moulds that he bought on a flea market. The screen in one of his rooms also has a story attached to it. Verlinden discovered this fine specimen at a jumble sale. It had been used by a travelling theatre company as a prop.

The house has a romantic patio garden. What used to be a rather ordinary lawn has now become a dolomite-strewn terrace lined with yews. Verlinden has planted many sweet-scented shrubs here that give off an exquisite fragrance on summer evenings.

After a stay in New England, Vincent Verlinden decided to go and live in the country. Traces of American influence can be found in his house, for instance the high plinths, the light-coloured panelling and the strip of wallpaper. The result is a cheerful and relaxing interior (left).

Although Vincent is not a collector, he often visits flea markets and auctions where he picks up the oddest things, including his favourite decoration, a screen (above) which was once used by a travelling theatre company as a prop. This curio does not really have a function, but it is an amusing eye-catcher.

LIFE
IN THE CITY

———

Flemish towns are full of towers offering a splendid view of the houses. In smaller towns like Bruges the scale of the panorama unfolding below is just perfect. This is a view (right) from the Gruuthuse mansion. Various styles of architecture, from Gothic to Art Nouveau, have gone to create a single whole.

THINKING OF FLEMISH towns I do not see the majestic boulevards lined with plane trees that are so typical of France. True, streets like these can be found in Brussels or Lille, cities that looked up to Paris. But truly Flemish towns evoke an image of narrow, twisting streets and alleys with a mixed architecture of large town houses and modest, small homes. Rich and poor live next to each other. Monotonous terraces, so common in Holland, are rare. Each house has its own distinctive character, for the Flemish are staunch individualists. Houses with slender spout-gables alternate with bell-gabled or step-gabled houses. In Ghent and Antwerp even factories were embellished with ornamental frills. All of this means that Flemish towns sometimes seem disorganized and unplanned. This impression is wrong, however. In Ghent, where archeologists are unravelling the earliest stages of town-building, they have discovered that building activities were preceded by a certain amount of planning. In the eleventh century tradesmen did not simply buy a plot of land near the local castle; streets were laid out first and land allotted. Large mansions were built on these sites, for wealthy citizens tried to emulate the nobility. It was only later, after the Battle of the Golden Spurs in 1302, that more modest houses made their appearance. Still, it is true that medieval cities such as Antwerp, Leuven or Mechelen lack the strict planning of towns like Tongeren, founded by the Romans.

The labyrinthine layout of the streets has a peculiar charm; it is easy to lose your way. You never know exactly where you are going, as most of your surroundings are hidden from view owing to the tall houses. The taller they are, the richer the city. In Ghent, Antwerp and Leuven houses with up to four stories were built. Accordingly, you cannot see any churchtowers unless you are right in front of them. Occasionally small shops were added on to a church, as a kind of annexe. Some of them can still be found in Ghent and Antwerp.

People looking for peace and quiet should visit one of the many almshouses. Halfway down a street you will suddenly come upon a gateway opening onto a courtyard with small houses, built for the elderly, grouped around it. Almshouses are like islands in the heart of towns. Every Flemish town, even small ones like Diksmuide or Diest, has a beguinage as well, which is a world unto itself. Each beguinage has a central courtyard with narrow alleys leading to it. Invariably, a large church stands in its centre. The only thing that is missing is a market place, because the beguines were not allowed to engage in trade.

Unlike Holland, Flanders is not a country dominated by water, but even so many rivers make their way through its clayey soil. The North Sea would reclaim a large part of the country if the Flemish had not built dikes to protect their polders against the repeated attacks of the water. When you see a river like the Durme winding peacefully through the countryside in summer it is hard to imagine how violent it will become later in the year. But with the approach of autumn the attack on the fragile dikes begins once again.

Almost all Flemish towns are built on estuaries or riverbanks. The River Zwin, formerly connecting Bruges with the sea, silted up long ago. But the small rivers running from Ghent to Bruges and Ostend were later transformed into beautiful canals, twisting and winding their way through the flat countryside that Jacques Brel has praised in song.

Ghent and Antwerp are, of course, dominated by the River Scheldt. In Antwerp you are constantly reminded of the sea by the ocean-going ships moving slowly past. Further inland, towards Brussels, you encounter the Brueghelian setting of a rolling countryside dotted with trees and picturesque villages.

Flemish towns take you back in time. The Middle Ages come to life again in Bruges, Damme, Veurne and Ghent. But Ghent especially is more than just a tribute to the past; it is also a sparkling university town. Antwerp is a major port with many different aspects. In Antwerp every era has created its own distinctive neighbourhood. Last century the massive Spanish fortifications were demolished. The Spanish castle on the waterfront was replaced by new docks and warehouses. Later the docks were filled in again and many of the warehouses were converted to art galleries. This part of Antwerp reminds you of New York's SoHo. Elsewhere in the city, in the suburb of Berchem, we find the Cogels Osy district, built at the turn of the century and a showpiece of the *belle époque*. A diversity of architectural styles and fashions, enriched with flamboyant touches of Art Nouveau, have gone into the creation of this upper middle-class neighbourhood. Fortunately, it was saved from destruction during the heyday of property development in the sixties.

The construction of the Cogels Osy district in Antwerp, around 1900, must have been a perplexing event. All of a sudden tall houses resembling creamcakes rose up among peacefully grazing cattle. The entire area is a splendid and beautifully preserved mixture of Neo-styles, sprinkled with flamboyant Art Nouveau. It is unique in Europe.

Almost every Flemish town has a beguinage, a secluded area with narrow lanes, squares and a church with small houses grouped around it. Beguinages were religious communities of spinsters and widows. They originated in the late twelfth century. Many of them have survived unchanged until the present day. The most beautiful beguinages are those of Ghent, Kortrijk, Hoogstraten, Lier, Leuven and Diest.

The beguinage of Bruges is set apart from the world by a stretch of water and by high walls with two gates that are closed at night. There is a convent, as well as houses for the elderly. It is particularly attractive in spring, when the daffodils in the garden are flowering. Many towns have almshouses as well. They resemble small beguinages and were built in the Middle Ages to provide shelter for the elderly. A large number can be found in Bruges, hidden behind an old wall or a small gateway.

When restoring the house Jan discovered this five-century-old fireplace (above and opposite). It is a work of art, for the lintel is decorated with a sculpted hunting scene. Many medieval fireplaces can still be found in Bruges, but they have rarely been decorated so opulently. The sides are decorated as well, showing the faces of a man and a woman. Jan Broes is fascinated by medieval art. He is fortunate to live in Bruges, where so many medieval houses remain. Jan keeps a close watch on any restoration work going on. When renovating a house, he says, you should be aware of the charm and uniqueness of wear and tear. The simple, but sophisticated furnishings are evidence that this is the house of someone with a passion for architecture. The starkness of the interior enables you to admire the building all the more. There is an open space in the centre (right) with a simple stairway leading to the first floor. Wherever you look, you can see inscribed stone objects or calligraphic drawings.

The column is just one of many such objects that Jan has brought home with him from his travels through Bruges. The tiles laid out in a checkered pattern in his garden were each collected in the same way. Every day he takes his bicycle to visit building sites, looking for newly discovered murals or sculptures. Old cities like Bruges are, after all, veritable treasure troves.

The church tile engraved by Lamborot is just one of many inscribed artefacts in Jan Broes' home. Stone objects with words carved in them are everywhere – hardly surprising, considering that once every three years Jan organizes an international calligraphy exhibition in his own home.

The garden at the back of the house is a green oasis, enclosed by high walls. Scattered among the boulders wisteria and hydrangea are flowering and there is an impressive box hedge. In the drawing room overlooking the garden the showpiece is a monumental fireplace whose mantel is decorated with a hunting scene. It is one of the most beautiful and original mantelpieces of Bruges – which is saying something, considering that so many fireplaces have been preserved in this city. The sides are decorated as well and show the faces of a man and a woman. No doubt this used to be the main room of the house, where meals were cooked and people spent most of their time.

The house has been restored in a remarkably subtle fashion. When renovating an old building, Jan Broes says, you should be aware of the charm and uniqueness of wear and tear. Jan is convinced that medieval houses were far more colourful than we now tend to think and refers to some recently discovered murals to support this opinion. He plans to add colour to his house, enriching it. The oak beams have already been painted a vivid green. Every once in a while you have to change things a bit, Jan Broes argues, because houses like these should be alive.

In the living room there is an antique display case full of bric-a-brac, including old keys, delftware, pottery shards from the garden and old wine bottles. This shrine contains the souvenirs and mementoes of an entire life. They are not precious objects but simple trinkets filled with memories. In the windowsill, for instance, are four large stones, fished up from some French river. Perhaps they have a symbolic value, for it seems likely that such stones polished clean by the water were the first things man collected.

A green oasis, enclosed by high walls, with an age-old floor. It has taken Jan many years to collect these paving stones. He found them on building sites where they were thrown away. At the far end of the garden is a small house with in front of it a stone inscribed with a quotation from Marcus Aurelius, 'Though you should break your heart, the people will continue like before'.

127

An imposing façade in a distinguished street. You have to walk up a few steps before you can enter. It is not a medieval house and yet it looks like a ship, with a flagpole for its bowsprit. The furnishings are casual. Anna found the antique Caucasian carpets, and Jan the architectural odds and ends. Places to sit and read are everywhere; even the entrance hall (opposite) has a bookcase. The living room (next page) looks Baroque and wintry; it is also used as a music room.

ARCHITECT JAN VANDEWALLE lives in Sint-Jansstraat, once Bruges' wealthiest street. Together with Ridderstraat, just around the corner, this was were the first merchants built their homes, near the castle. Today, it is a quiet street with unremarkable houses, but it has retained an atmosphere of distinction. In the eighteenth century, during the time of Austrian rule, most of the medieval fronts were covered with plaster to make them look modern and more distinguished. Jan and Anna Vandewalle's house, which was built in the early nineteenth century, also has a severe classical façade. Jan and Anna had been trying for years to find a suitable house in this part of town when they chanced upon this fine building. It had been in use as an office for more than fifty years, so that both its exterior and its interior had been well maintained.

When Jan and Anna saw this house with its many possibilities they fell at once in love with it. They created seating areas everywhere, even in the entrance hall. The hall itself looks like a winter garden, with its bookcase and many plants. The living-room area has been divided into a summer and a winter room. The bright summer room contains books about art and architecture; the darker winter room with its large fireplace is distinctly Baroque in character, which Anna likes. It contains seventeenth-century furniture as well as a china cabinet and a grand piano. It is also used as a music room. A friend from Paris, a pianist who loves Bruges, frequently stays with Jan and Anna and will then give private concerts for a few intimates.

At first Jan and Anna intended to convert and modernize their house. It is a good thing that they changed their minds. Jan's respect for the architecture of the past has grown considerably. He now feels that modern creations, no matter how beautiful, lack the warmth of old houses. Hence the Vandewalle's prefer-

ence for old materials and decorations. In this way they try to leave the weight of the ages undisturbed.

What is especially exciting about old houses is that they make you speculate about their history. This house goes back a long way – the side walls may be more than four hundred years old. It used to have a wooden front, which was pulled down to reduce the risk of fire. In the eighteenth century towns would pay subsidies to home-owners to replace wooden fronts by brick or stone façades. Around 1780 the interior was renovated (right). The oak beams were hidden behind plaster and the Gothic fireplaces replaced by elegant marble mantels. The winter garden (opposite) is a delight. It is surely the most intriguing part of the house. Behind the arches is an old larder containing antique china and silverware.

A SHORT DISTANCE further along Sint-Jansstraat Corinne Stuckens lives in a step-gabled house. Step-gables are not, of course, peculiar to Bruges, for they can be seen anywhere in Flanders. But in Bruges an exceptionally large number of them have been preserved. Perhaps this is why the people of Bruges like them so much – step-gabled houses bring them closer to the medieval past of their city.

Corinne's house reminds you of an old sailing ship because its interior is almost entirely made of wood. It used to have a wooden front as well, but the façade was pulled down in the early eighteenth century, probably because it was in bad repair. The builder must have been a wealthy man, but he did not like ornamentation. The façade is almost Spartan in its austerity. The interior is simple as well. The wooden beams were covered by plaster, at that time a very modern touch. The fireplace was decorated with stucco in the rather imposing Louis-seize style, also known as *à la Grecque*. All the features of classical architecture are present. The fireplace in the front room was embellished with a garden vase and a cornucopia; this room was no doubt used as a dining room. Musical instruments – a violin, trumpet and pan flute – adorn the fireplace in the back room, perhaps indicating that the people who lived here were musicians.

Corinne has subtly restored her house, changing hardly anything. She even left the flooring and piping intact, feeling that an old house should not look perfect. She refreshed the interior, furnishing it in a simple style. A few easy chairs and a dinner table constitute most of the furniture. The bookcase is made of an old display case picked up in a shop and painted white. The predominatingly bright colours give the house a modern appearance.

The winter garden strikes the imagination. Until

recently the grand piano of the previous owner was kept here. Now it is Corinne's favourite dining room. The old-fashioned glass roof lets in bright sunlight even in winter.

ANYONE WHO LIKES picture postcards will at once feel at home in Dominique Desimpel's apartment. His pied-à-terre in Bruges looks out on two unique views. Through one window you can see the majestic Belfry, the huge tower keeping watch over Bruges like a medieval knight. Another window looks out on the River Dyver and Rozenhoedkaai and provides a dramatic view of a finely balanced ensemble of towers, bridges and trees. The apartment is situated in a remarkable building above an arched gallery. Dominique has furnished his home with a Dutch cabinet, an English méridienne and a French Empire table. The chairs, by the designer Tom Dixon, match this warm interior perfectly. Dominique used to be a keen collector of Tournai china and uses his superb collection every day. The white chinaware with its delicate blue glazing goes exceptionally well with the mahogany furniture. By now, this interior may have undergone a complete transformation. Dominique changes it once every month and repaints his apartment in a different colour once every year.

This remarkable building suddenly looms up from behind other houses to enjoy a unique view of the city (above). Its architect used an old-fashioned but very charming solution to prevent it from blocking the road: he built an arched gallery over the pavement.

Someone once called Dominique's bachelor's pad very appropriately 'A Room with a View'. The first thing visitors will do is stand at the window and look at the townscape. The heavy drapes deliberately keep part of the view out. Odd as it may sound, this picture postcard scene is almost too beautiful for comfort.

This house stands on a corner along an eighteenth-century canal, the Coupure, in Ghent. Originally this was a district of factories and workshops, but from 1860 onwards mansions were built on the banks of the canal. The house, in a typical Classicistic style, has a roofed carriage porch. Olivier Neyrinck restored it with great care. The decorations are by Agnès Emery, who has done an excellent job. The interior breathes the atmosphere of the fin de siècle. Much as people did a century ago, she has mixed elements from a variety of cultures and periods. Agnès is from Brussels, the capital of Art Nouveau, and it shows. Small mats with Morris designs hang in the windows.

THIS HOUSE SHOWS that Agnès Emery, its decorator, has an intellectual relationship with William Morris. Before she she discovered Morris, she had a similar relationship with that other celebrity, Josef Hoffmann. Her ties with Hoffmann date from her childhood, when she often visited the Palais Stoclet in Brussels, Hoffmann's masterpiece, as a friend of one of the children of the family who lived there. This Art Nouveau monument and Klimt's mysterious frescoes caught her imagination at once. Agnès had a marvellous grandfather who used to buy Liberty silk for his granddaughters to make clothes from. She once posed for him in a dress of this lovely material.

William Morris inspired her with a love of colourful ornaments. Although she qualified as an architect she never, to my knowledge, designed a house, preferring Owen Jones, the father of the Arts and Crafts movement, to Le Corbusier, the idol of her generation. Loos, who argued that ornaments were criminal, she rejected without further thought.

By now, Agnès has provided many buildings with deep, mysterious colours. A good example of her work is L'Amadeus, one of Brussels' best-known restaurants, which she decorated in collaboration with the owner, Christian Neyrinck, another unorthodox architect.

The interior of this house in Ghent, belonging to Christian's brother Olivier, clearly shows the influence of the *Wiener Sezession* style. The dining room is an extension of the linear flooring and the black-marble fireplace. Agnès painted the dark walls with a frieze of green palm fronds. All the rooms have been given a different character, creating an effect of surprise. The sitting room is a tribute to the *belle époque*. In one corner Agnès had a huge niche built, full of soft cushions with oriental patterns. She got this idea in Provence, where couches used to be put in an alcove. This is the origin of the *radassière*, a word derived from Provençal *radassa*, meaning to laze about, to be idle.

The bedroom shows the influence of William Morris' native country. Agnès painted luxuriant vines on ordinary striped wallpaper. The walls are hung with antique prints in gilt frames. In the world of decorators and architects Agnès is something of an odd woman out. She uses a lot of recycled materials, for instance, including tiles and Art Nouveau faience. When she began doing this, years ago, there used to be a huge supply because so many beautiful houses have been pulled down in Belgium.

The ensemble was painted in faux-bois. The word radassière derives from Provençal radassa, meaning 'to laze, to be idle'.
While Agnès Emery's fellow-students idolized Le Corbusier, she studied the works of Morris, Hoffmann and Owen Jones. Loos, who held that ornaments were criminal, she rejected without a second thought. This mysterious dining room (opposite) proves that people can do without the austerity of Functionalism.

This entrance hall used to look quite different, as it was painted in the usual drab grey. But Agnès Emery likes using colours. The powerful blue is an excellent match for the black marble stairway and the Art Deco floor. Every room in this house has been given a different colour scheme.
Agnès furnished the sitting room with a radassière, or Turkish sofa, to the left of the fireplace. It is really a kind of raised platform, draped with cushions and built into a recess in the wall. The two columns supporting the cornice above the sofa she bought from an antiques dealer.

140

TO REACH THIS
sumptuous interior you
have to find your way
through a series of narrow streets
and alleys in Ghent, hardly wide
enough for a car. When you finally
get there, however, the surprise may
be so great that you will be hard put
to find your way back. Once this
was the warehouse of a piano
factory, where parts of musical
instruments lay scattered across the
floor and a divine light shone
through the lofty windows. But
this tall, narrow building seemed
destined for demolition, since no-one
was interested in it. Until its present
owner moved in. A lot of planning
has gone into making this rabbit-
warren fit to live in again, with
amazing results. The magnificent
dining room is just ten feet wide, but
you hardly notice how narrow it is,
as the lavish decorations claim all
your attention. Beyond the dining
room the library and sitting room at
once catch the eye. The interior is
emphatically decorative and meant
to impress visitors, as the enormous
drapes show. But despite this
bourgeois ostentation the old factory
warehouse unmistakably makes its
presence felt. That is what
constitutes the mysterious charm of
this fine house.

144

The bedroom (left) is almost directly over the Empire room, but apart from the fireplace, which also dates from the Empire period, it has been furnished in a completely different style. The dark red walls create an atmosphere of warmth. But both rooms have one thing in common – their austerity. There is not even a carpet on the floor. In a corner you can glimpse an antique bath-tub. The bathroom, too, is beautiful and unpretentious (right). Every single thing, from the bath-tub to the mirror, was bought from antiques dealers. The floor tiles, the wooden linen cupboard and the oil-painted walls provide the finishing touch. Harmony and simplicity prevail here. The kitchen (above) was completely redesigned by architect Paul Robbrecht.

THIS LOFT COULD
equally well have been
situated in New York or
London. But actually it is located in
an Antwerp warehouse dating from
the twenties, a time when Antwerp
had close links with many overseas
ports. Ocean liners and freighters
would come and go, transporting
people and cargo from the old world
to the new. It was an era when The
International Style and Art Deco
flourished in Antwerp. The use of
concrete supports and iron window
frames gave an industrial look to
many residential buildings.

Architect Vincent Van Duysen,
who lives here, has hardly changed the
interior at all and has not even redecorated the walls and ceilings. He has
chosen highly sophisticated, bright furnishings, however, which is hardly
surprising, because like his mentor,
Jean De Meulder, he spent a long time
in Italy.

'I don't intend to compose really new tunes,' Jean De Meulder says prosaically. 'When you listen to Charlie Parker or Miles Davis you recognize their sound, rather than the music they play.' The same thing goes for interior decorating, he feels, for only in this way will a particular style become timeless. He rarely copies from design catalogues, but designs most of his furniture himself, including that in his dining room (left). The rear façade of his house is painted black, evidence of his lengthy stay in New York.

B ECAUSE OF ITS
high degree of indutria-
lization, Ghent is some-
times called the Manchester of the
Continent. At the end of the
eighteenth century even the medieval
Gravensteen castle was transformed
into a cotton mill. The first
'fireproof' factories came from
Manchester. Before 1800 most
factories had been built of wood, but
then cast iron began to be used to
reduce the risk of fire.
These old factories are now being
converted to dwelling houses and
studios. Ludovic Devriendt's loft is a
workroom rather than a dwelling.
Ludovic, who is a landscape
gardener, lives on the third floor of
a factory from 1927 in Perkament-
straat in Ghent. The building is
situated in the town centre and has a
splendid view of the city's rooftops.
The interior has been sparely and
simply furnished, underlining its
bond with the austere factory
architecture.

OLD WAREHOUSES are mostly transformed into luxurious lofts with spare interiors. But decorators Marc Vergauwe and Jan Rosseel preferred a less obvious approach. In Ghent they discovered a linen warehouse, built in 1860 on top of one of the town's old fortifications, and remodelled it as an eighteenth-century maison de plaisance. Mostly they live in the impressive kitchen, which would not be out of place in a mansion. They took out one of the floors, thus creating an immensely high ceiling, which enabled them to put in the tall Dutch windows. The stucco decorations on the walls are another reference to Daniel Marot, the Dutch Frenchman. The care with which Marc and Jan proceed is also manifest in the kitchen cupboards that were painstakingly copied from authentic models and look genuinely old. Marc and Jan look to the past for inspiration, but they create interiors that are unmistakably part of this fin de siècle era. Hence their collecting mania, for they gather anything they can find, including old window glass, as if the things of the past may disappear with the onset of the new millennium. They may well be right, considering how many charming and decorative objects, though not really valuable or antique, are lost.

ARTISTS AND COLLECTORS

———

FLEMISH ARTISTS and collectors have close ties. Nor are they all that different, considering that a good many artists are keen collectors themselves. Pieter Paul Rubens, for instance, was a great admirer of antique bronze and marble busts. As befitted his status as a gentleman he also collected works by old masters and contemporary artists, but cheap trinkets were taboo. True, he did own some curios, including a mummy – but that was a rare object which probably cost him a fortune. If Rubens had survived until the early years of this century he might have visited the studio of his fellow-artist Baron James Ensor in Ostend. What a shock that would have been ! Rather than surrounding himself with the works of famous painters, Ensor collected dried sea monsters, carnival masks and rare shells. Rubens would have been hard put to keep his composure in the presence of Beelzebub, who sits at Ensor's living-room table, disguised as an old fisherwoman. Visitors used to be rather subdued by this scary monster, failing to appreciate the surrealistic atmosphere of the house. Some, however, were more intrepid, like the painter Vasily Kandinsky who once sat at this table enjoying a nice cup of tea with the Master.

Ensor's living room with its pompous marble fireplace and flowery wallpaper is typically bourgeois. But the weird masks on the dresser, the piano and the sofa seem to mock their middle-class surroundings. On top of a pile of books is a Chinese ginger jar crowned with a skull and the flowery hat Ensor wore in one of his self-portraits. The blue room where Ensor painted and composed is a *tableau vivant* full of bizarre props. Sitting underneath the huge canvas of *The Entry of Christ into Brussels* he would play his *Gamme d'amour* on the harmonium.

At the circular table next to Beelzebub he would write virulent letters and speeches dealing with artists, critics and politicians. Architects and property developers he contemptuously referred to as 'one-eyed financiers, hollow speculators and turd-shaped roadbuilders'.

In this house, which he inherited in 1917 from one of his uncles, he created a universe of his own. He never changed anything. The novelty shop housed his curio collection. It is full of ship's models, dried sea monsters and trashy souvenirs. The fans, Chinese lanterns and other *chinoiseries* he got from Tan Hee Tsen, a Chinese who married his sister Mitche in 1892. This oriental gentleman, who walked around Ostend dressed in a skirt and with his hair in plaits, soon returned to his native country, leaving a small daughter behind.

During the *belle époque* Ostend was a somewhat bizarre town, whose streets were populated with all sorts of odd people, including several village idiots. Ensor himself was a rather striking figure as well. People used to call him 'the walking statue', because he would invariably dress in a black jacket, a large bow tie and a matching little hat. The suit he wore when meeting Einstein in 1933 still hangs from a peg in the office behind the shop. The artist merged perfectly with his background, for Ostend was an unusual town with big-city aspirations and an international atmosphere. A remarkably large number of wealthy Eastern European Jews had settled there.

Most of the large town houses of that era have now gone. Only a few have been preserved. Visitors can still follow in the footsteps of Ensor, however. His house, which was turned into a museum many years ago, is, of course, the main attraction. But Ostend has a number of other fine historical buildings, including the royal stables. This wooden structure, dating from 1904, was designed by the Norwegian architect Knutsen and built in Scandinavian style.

People tend to think that the interior of Kosuth's house is rather frigid. But they are wrong. It is a comfortable home for people who enjoy life. And yet, the interior is somewhat unusual. Here and there it seems empty, as a result of the bare floor and unadorned walls. The winged angel and the lone landscape painting provide a touch of surrealism.

The house shows traces of a distant past. The mantelpiece dates from the eighteenth century, the frescoes on the ceiling from around 1880. In a corner of one of the rooms part of the original stairway was discovered. A trompe l'oeil is all that remains. It matches this interior perfectly.

THE AMERICAN ARTIST Joseph Kosuth lives immediately behind the eighteenth-century Hôtel Verhaegen in Ghent. His own house is just as deeply rooted in the past, for its oldest walls are more than two hundred years old. Situated in a back alley, it can hardly be seen from the street. But behind its simple façade are a spacious interior and a magnificent garden.

Joseph Kosuth commutes between Ghent and New York, where he has another pied-à-terre. Jan Hoet, the curator of the Ghent Museum of Contemporary Art, invited Kosuth to Ghent on the occasion of his prestigious Chambres d'Amis exhibition in 1986. It is thanks to the efforts of Hoet, who also organized Documenta 92 in Kassel in Germany, that Ghent now has a large public interested in modern art. Kosuth feels completely at home here.

For the Chambres d'Amis exhibition Kosuth painted a text on the wall of an interior, then crossed it out; it was a paragraph from Sigmund Freud's *The Psychopathology of Everyday Life*. In his own home you won't see such things. There are some works by modern masters, but overall the interior has a timeless atmosphere. Most of the old-fashioned decorations were carefully restored, including the painted ceilings and a mural. They betray the influence of Kosuth's wife, art historian Cornelia Lauf.

Just two rooms in Jan Van Looveren's apartment contain no books: the kitchen and the workshop. In a corner of the kitchen is a lighted globe, set among a few bottles. You cannot help wondering why it is here. Globes, after all, tend to be put in libraries. They also symbolize travel. Although Jan is not an adventurer, he travels a lot, both in space and in time. His books take him to the far corners of the earth.
Jan has surrounded himself with exquisite objects which he displays ingeniously. A good example are the fine monochrome vases with yellow glazing. These showpieces from the thirties were manufactured by Boch La Louvière.

RESTORER Jan Van Looveren has several mottoes, but the one he prefers is *Living well is the best revenge*. I suspect him of a tendency to distance himself from the world. It shows when you enter his apartment: high above the street, it is like an island set apart from the rest of the city. Gravensteen, Ghent's medieval castle, is just a stone's throw away. Van Looveren has converted what used to be maid's rooms into an exceptionally snug living area. Books are everywhere. Van Looveren is a keen reader – 'Books are my best friends', he says – with a preference for literary fiction. He feels that interior decoration is a much underrated subject. Art historians will write lengthy treatises about architecture and antiquities, but they rarely discuss interiors. Van Looveren argues that the furnishings of a house tell more about the life-style of the inhabitants than anything else. The description of a room in a novel by Zola or Balzac lets you know at once what kind of people you are dealing with, up to the point of being able to guess at their ambitions, habits and family traditions.

Van Looveren's interior has a classical, quiet look, but it is not at all dull. He never experiments with freakish shapes or unusual colours and is imaginative enough to arrange old objects in a light-hearted manner. The decorations are a colourful mixture of various styles. A much-travelled man, he has brought home several charming souvenirs. His travels have even influenced the colour scheme of his house. When he returned from a journey to Ecuador he decided to repaint his kitchen in red.

Jan's restoration workshop looks completely different, of course. Although he did not really decorate this workroom, everything has its place here, including the Chinese letters on the wall. Nothing will disturb him here, so that he can work at ease.

171

Missenburg estate has been a family domain for a long time. It is a stone's throw from Antwerp and has miraculously been left untouched by the twentieth century. The writer Marie Gevers wrote her impressionistic novels here; her son, the poet Paul Willems, today continues that literary tradition. The library on the first floor has a splendid view of the wild garden with its age-old trees. Paul's father once painted a series of twelve watercolours, portraying the same spot in the garden at different times of the year. They are hung in the former dining room, which has largely remained unchanged in the past century.

'WHEN MY GRANDFATHER was forty years old, he decided to retire from business,' says poet Paul Willems. At a time when Belgium was rapidly approaching the Second Industrial Revolution, Floris Gevers, an admirer of Jean-Jacques Rousseau, went in search of the peace and quiet of country life. When he decided to buy Missenburg, a farmer warned him that the house was haunted by the ghost of a highwayman called Guldentop. The estate had been left temporarily vacant after the French Revolution, until the highwayman moved in. When he was finally caught, he was sentenced to death, becoming the last person to lose his head under the guillotine in Antwerp. According to legend, Saint Peter did not want to let him enter heaven unless he returned the money he had stolen. But having lost his memory as a result of being beheaded, he was doomed to roam the corridors of Missenburg, looking for his treasure. Undaunted by this story, Floris Gevers, a firm believer in the intrinsic goodness of man, bought the estate regardless and made friends with the ghost. Missenburg thus remains a halfway house between heaven and earth.

The new owner surrounded Missenburg by a thick wall of greenery, separating it from the world. The estate became fully self-sufficient. The last pear of the previous year's harvest would be eaten together with the first cherries of the new season. The children did not attend school, but were taught from the *Aventures de Télémaque*, a study book used by the French educationalist Fénelon to teach King Louis XV.

Books rather than leaves should grow from the trees in the park. Writing is a way of life for the people of Missenburg, who have described everything you see in the tiniest detail. Floris Gevers' daughter Marie wrote several books here at the turn of the century. In her *Vie et mort d'un étang* she subtly portrays the house and its

environment, expressing the poetry of wind, rain, seasons and silence by writing, 'Ecoute mieux, on entend un bruit léger, léger...c'est le temps qui passe.' Paul Neuhaus, Roger Avermaet, Georges Duhamel, Paul Delvaux, Emile Verhaeren and many other friends of the family visited Missenburg to enjoy its blissful tranquillity. Today Paul Willems, Marie's son, lives here. He has carefully kept everything in its original state. Even Marie Gevers' old desk-cum-bookcase is still here, with all her writings in it. The desk and the books have been donated to the National Library but will remain in the house for as long as her descendants live here.

Paul's father spent much of his time in the garden. Some of the shrubs are more than three hundred years old. The garden also has many rare fruit trees with poetic names such as *Beurré Hardy*, *Seigneur d'Esperen*, *Louise bonne d'Avranche* and *Joséphine de Malines*. Paul's father portrayed this poetic environment in a series of fine watercolours now adorning the living room. There are twelve of them, one for each month of the year. The same tree is shown in all of them, its leaves, branches and roots smoothly blending in the best traditions of English watercolouring. In Missenburg all mementoes are lovingly cherished. Rousseau would have felt happy here.

Before Kaat Tilley moved into this small castle, it was used as a school. A long time ago it was the residence of an aristocratic family. The central part of the building dates from the Middle Ages. At one time it may have been the country home of wealthy people from Brussels or Mechelen, who came here to enjoy the summer sun. The house is oriented towards the light. Most of the original decorations have gone. Kaat has restored the interior to her own taste, just putting in some garden furniture and leaving many empty spaces. There is no separate living room, for her studio is also where she lives. In this house work and play are inextricably intertwined.

FASHION DESIGNER Kaat Tilley left Brussels to return to the tranquillity of her native village, Kapelle-op-den-Bos. It was not a move that she ever expected would happen – until she got the opportunity of buying a large, romantic house with an English garden, a hermitage and an ice cellar. A few hundred years ago Coninckxsteen, as the house is called, was the country residence of wealthy people from Brussels or Mechelen. Its turrets show its link with the distant past. Not much of the interior has been preserved. Kaat lives and works in the two turrets, having painted the walls herself. She asked furniture designer Dirk Meylaerts to make her a round desk, fitting the shape of the turret. One floor up she reserves a room for friends from the city who want to find a moment's peace here.

Half an hour's driving will take you from the heart of Brussels to this dreamhouse, set in a five-acre domain. For many generations people have come from Brussels to find peace and quiet in the green areas surrounding the city.

EDOUARD VERMEULEN, a fashion designer, decided to change his apartment in Brussels for an eighteenth-century country home in Sint-Katelijne-Waver. A wise decision, because in the metropolis he had hardly any time to enjoy life. In his new home he can relax. It is an ideal environment for designing new fashions. With Brussels just twenty miles away, half an hour's drive will take Vermeulen to a dreamlike landscape.

Rozenhout estate used to be a country retreat, a precursor of our present-day villas. Houses like these were not permanently occupied but used as summer residences. Rozenhout was probably built for a wealthy Brussels family. It dates from the time of Austrian rule, when exaggerated French flamboyance was softened by Classicistic touches. The house is not built on a monumental scale, but constructed along more human proportions, which its present owner prefers. Vermeulen does not like opulent decors. Rather than being set in the middle of a park, the house is built on the edge of a wood. It has a beautiful view of green trees and shrubs. Vermeulen first restored the garden and then the house itself. With its light colours the interior radiates a summer atmosphere. Although it was repainted, nothing else was changed in order to preserve the original features. Vermeulen feels that houses should never be fully restored and that signs of wear and tear should remain visible.

At the far end of the house we find Leo's bedroom. Here you can see that he has worked in old buildings for many years. He loves painted wooden sculptures. The small rocaille above the nightstand is his favourite. The large black frames came from a church and were thrown away years ago. Leo intends to make paintings for them.

Each room breathes a different atmosphere because Leo has used a variety of colour schemes and sticks to appropriate furniture. Kitchen cupboards belong in the dining room (left), not in the living room. It is as simple as that. But don't think that this interior was created in a single day. It took Leo many years.

Leo has spent his life among paint tubes, brushes and palette knives. This is his studio-cum-living room. The actual living room of the house serves as a kind of entrance hall. Leo is more than just an ornamental painter. Like his father and grandfather before him, he also paints on canvas. He has produced both figurative and abstract work. Most of the paintings in his house were made by himself.

Their interest in gilt leather is a coincidence, for originally they restored old windows. When they were asked to repair a set of antique gilt leather sheets, they became interested in this fine material. Making gilt leather requires a lot of preparation. Lut (above) makes the design and engraves it in wax. The wax model is used to make the bronze mould. Frederic finishes the gilt with colour and varnish. The result is a beautiful sheet of calfskin measuring 27 by 31 inches. A sheet like this is called a 'samson'.

AFTER MANY YEARS of experimenting, Lut and Frederic Poppe from Ghent have succeeded in producing gilt leather again. International interest in this unique type of wall covering is constantly growing. Following a long article in *The World of Interiors* Lut and Frederic were approached by many enthusiasts in both Europe and the USA.

Lut and Frederic had to reinvent the art of making gilt leather as people had long ago stopped making this product. Fortunately, in the Mechelen Records Office they found a unique seventeenth-century document, called the *Book of Secrets concerning Diverse Beautiful Arts and Crafts Discovered by Jan Vermeulen, Gilt Leather Maker of the City of Mechelen*. Mechelen was a major European production centre of gilt leather in the seventeenth and eighteenth centuries. Vermeulen was a scion of a renowned family of gilt leather makers. From his book Lut and Frederic got what they needed to start making gilt leather again. Like their predecessors, they use bronze moulds to shape the leather. Designing the moulds is an art in itself. Lut first makes a wax model that Frederic turns into a plaster form used to produce the bronze cast.

Oddly enough, silver is used to gilt the leather rather than gold. The silver is coloured and varnished by Frederic, whose skills enable him to give the finished product an age-old patina. It is hardly possible to keep an antique and a contemporary sample apart. The Poppes use seventeenth- and eighteenth-century motifs. Their handiwork can be used to considerable effect for restorations or in a period interior. Perhaps Flemish gilt leather will one day be exported again all over the world.

A careful observer will discover quite a lot of old wrought iron in Flemish towns. Cramp irons, for instance, adorn the front of every old house. Sometimes they are little more than straightforward metal bars, but even such simple black lines have a decorative effect. On many houses the cramp irons have been shaped into elegant numerals. Medieval houses have iron rings to support long wooden poles used for hanging laundry from. Finally, there are the many balconies, especially those belonging to eighteenth-century houses. All these things were made of wrought iron, forged by blacksmiths using hammer and anvil.

IN A NARROW ALLEY behind the Beguinage of Bruges stands an old industrial building that clearly shows the ravages of time. Its location in this picturesque area beloved by tourists makes it all the more conspicuous. From the street you can hear the sound of people labouring away inside. The building houses the Van den Abeele blacksmith's shop. In the centre of the smithy is a huge receptacle full of glowing embers heating the iron to be beaten into shape. Over the years all kinds of ornamental ironwork have come from this place, ranging from wrought-iron gates to signposts. The attic contains the heritage of five generations of blacksmiths. The Van den Abeele story began last century, when Johannes-Franciscus set up his forge. Pierre, the present incumbent, conscientiously continues the family tradition. Many of his ancestors were highly talented. In the twenties Julien Van den Abeele crafted graceful eagles, storks, owls and serpents, subtly fashioned in iron. These animal figures are part of a great tradition of Belgian animaliers, whose most prominent representative was Rembrandt Bugatti.

P EOPLE OFTEN ASSOCIATE delftware with Holland and forget that this type of earthenware originated in Flanders. In the sixteenth century many Italian potters emigrated to Antwerp, Bruges, Ghent and Mechelen, where they made these blue-and-white tiles. After the Fall of Antwerp in 1585 and the partition of the Low Countries they travelled North, setting up new firms in Middelburg, Rotterdam and Delft. But Flemish potteries continued to operate throughout the seventeenth and eighteenth centuries.

Today, the most beautiful delft is not made in Holland, but in a workshop in Kortrijk. Father and son De Knock use old techniques, producing tiles with minor irregularities and crackled glaze, just as in the past. Collecting old tiles gave Paul De Knock the idea to start making delft himself. It took him many years to master the production process. Professional literature is scarce, many techniques have become extinct and some materials are no longer available. But now he is a past master at his job. His new delftware can hardly be distinguished from antique tiles. De Knock reuses many of the old decorations of craftsmen, children's games and ships. The firm also makes Torhout tiles, modelled after the tiles formerly made in this Flemish town. These are old-fashioned paving tiles and what are known as 'lion tiles', made of red-and-white clay.

This beautiful tile is the result of a life-long quest, involving a struggle with clay, fire and paint-brushes. It is an imitation of one of the oldest types of Flemish tiles. Around 1540 such majolica tiles were made in Antwerp by Italian expatriates. After the Fall of Antwerp in 1585 most of them went to Holland, where they settled in Delft and other towns and began manufacturing the celebrated blue-and-white delftware. More than two centuries separate the majolica tile from the traditional landscape with a windmill (above). Today, the most beautiful delftware is once again made in Flanders.

CHAPTER III
GARDENING

Flanders was once the leading horticultural nation of Europe. In the sixteenth century the Antwerp humanists turned Flanders into a centre of botany. In the eighteenth and nineteenth centuries dozens of fruit varieties were created and the rarest plants grown and improved. But every time war and foreign occupation put an end to this thriving gardening culture. In recent years we have witnessed a remarkable revival of gardening and beautiful new gardens are now once more created.

Mien Ruys, the influential Dutch gardening expert whose ideas have had an impact on several generations of Flemish gardeners as well, wrote 35 years ago, 'Whether gardens are ugly or beautiful does not really matter; it is certainly not a major concern. What is important is the way people use their gardens as an environment to live in. People who enjoy beauty will, of course, want their gardens to be beautiful, too. The crucial factor, then, is how people live in their gardens.'

THE GARDENS OF Flanders reflect the turbulent history of this part of Europe, which in the course of the centuries has been occupied by virtually every other European country. In the rest of Europe gardening followed an almost continuous evolution influenced by the successive styles and fashions of the major schools of architecture, but the history of Flemish gardening is one of alternate ups and downs. Periods of economic and cultural prosperity when gardening thrived were repeatedly followed by foreign occupation, war and famine, resulting in the wholesale destruction of many fine gardens.

Both culturally and geographically Flanders is a transitional region between the Latin and Northern worlds, between the exuberant South and the puritan North, between Catholic and Protestant Europe. More than anything else, it is all these different influences that have shaped the character of Flemish gardens with their diversity of styles – a diversity sometimes to be seen in a single garden. Flemish gardens are the horticultural expression of a multicultural society *avant la lettre*.

There is really no such thing as a typical Flemish gardening style. There is no Flemish counterpart to the classical gardens of France, the Renaissance gardens of Italy or the landscape and cottage gardens of Britain. Still, Flemish landscape gardeners have interpreted all these different styles in their own way, thus creating gardens that are, in a sense, uniquely Flemish. The last few decades have seen a marked revival of interest in gardening. Several Flemish landscape designers who have achieved international fame are now putting Flanders back on the gardening map, reminding us of the time when Flanders was Europe's leading gardening nation.

'ELEGANT GARDENS AND ORCHARDS OF DIFFERENT SHAPES FITTINGLY LAID OUT ACCORDING TO THE REQUIREMENTS OF ARCHITECTURE'

When Elizabeth, the sister of Emperor Charles V, had to leave her beloved Flanders to follow her husband to Denmark, she brought a whole army of Flemish gardeners with her. They set about draining swamps, turning them into fertile soil, and made Copenhagen the 'Garden of the North'.

There are many other such stories which illustrate the rich gardening history of Flanders. Charles V himself had a remarkable garden laid out in Brussels on the spot where the Royal Palace now stands. In 1556 he sent his Brussels gardener to San Yuste in Spain, ordering him to lay out another garden which he intended to take care of himself. His aunt, Margaret of Austria, governess of the Netherlands, had a garden laid out in Mechelen. When her castle, which now houses the district court, was restored a few years ago, the garden was restored as well, following a sixteenth-century model. Although the reconstruction is by no means historically accurate, it gives us at least some idea of what Flemish gardens of that era must have looked like.

The restored garden is very austere, but at the same time highly evocative. It has an almost meditative or mystical character and shows all the features of an enclosed medieval garden. Near the entrance are two symmetrical squares, each divided into four rectangular grass surfaces lined with box hedges. On the corners are yew columns and box globes. Further along are two more gardens of similar design. These have square compartments marked by box hedges. A circular fountain is set in the centre of one of these compartments, trimmed boxwood in the other. Grapevines have been trained along the walls. A striking feature of this garden is its lack of flowers.

A unique feature of the garden is its open-air theatre, consisting entirely of hornbeam and seating an audience of more than a thousand in separate green boxes around a central stage, a simple lawn. Plays like *Cyrano de Bergerac*, Corneille's *Le menteur* and Goethe's *Egmont* were performed here. The tradition is continued by the present residents. A few years ago Shakespeare's *As You Like It* was performed and during the Mozart Year works by this composer were played.

ORANGERIES

Leeuwergem has a beautiful orangery which was recently restored. It can be found next to the large enclosed vegetable garden.

In the eighteenth century, and even more so in the nineteenth century, orangeries were the dream of every rich garden owner. The emerging middle classes in particular, whose wealth derived from trade and manufacture, saw gardening and growing exotic plants as a way of displaying their riches and making their presence felt in a world which until then had been the preserve of aristocrats, bishops and scholars. Orangeries were the status symbol *par excellence*. Dozens of them have been preserved near Ghent and Antwerp, but most are in bad repair and need to be restored urgently.

Orangeries were not greenhouses but stone or brick structures with large south-facing windows where orange trees, laurels and other exotic plants could be kept in winter. Unlike conservatories and winter gardens, however, which were annexed to houses so that people could watch tropical plants even in winter, orangeries were usually built some distance away from a house as part of an enclosed garden. In winter they were heated to provide additional warmth when sunlight was scarce, and ingenious heating systems were often devised.

One of the most remarkable orangeries, unfortunately in very bad repair, is the one belonging to the Gavergracht estate, also known as Blauwhuys, in Vinderhoute. It was built in 1836 by Mr van de Woestyne-Clemmen, a rich manufacturer. First he had an orangery built on the southern side of his house (it was pulled down after World War I), but his passion for exotic plants was so great – he was one of the originators of the Ghent Flower Show – that he had another one built as well, on the northern side of the enclosed vegetable garden. Two shifts of at least five workers were required day and night to keep the ingenious heating system going permanently in winter!

Underneath this orangery is a semi-subterranean greenhouse where pineapples were grown. The growth of pineapples for consumption was a Flemish specialty until the middle of the nineteenth century. The interest in horticulture that began as a hobby of the rich aristocracy and middle classes of Ghent eventually developed into one of the main economic activities of the region and turned Ghent into a world centre of camellias, azaleas and begonias.

ORCHARDS

Before World War II ornamental gardens were the privilege of the wealthy middle classes, the aristocracy and the clergy, so that they were relatively rare. Growing fruit and vegetables, on the other hand, was an immensely popular activity among ordinary people in the eighteenth and nineteenth centuries. At one time every farmhouse in Flanders had an orchard. In front of every farm stood a hazel tree to keep insects away. And in the narrow strips of garden at the back of working-class houses at least a few fruit trees could be found. Until quite recently dozens of old orchards were cut down every year to make room for industrial zones or new housing developments. Others were replaced by far more productive dwarfing stocks producing modern types of fruit.

Fortunately, the renewed interest in gardening since the sixties and an increased ecological awareness have led to a revival of orchards with tall-stemmed trees. A growing number of gardening enthusiasts are creating new orchards with such trees, often selecting old fruit varieties that are threatened with extinction because of the increasing scale of commercial horticulture. In the province of Limburg, a centre of horticulture, the National Orchard Trust was established some years ago to try and save old orchards and promote the growth of old fruit varieties. Its catalogue lists 175 different apple trees, 100 pear trees and 72 plum trees.

Contemporary gardens are often too small to allow room for orchards. But it is perfectly possible to integrate fruit trees in an ornamental garden. The garden of the Van Oostveldt family in one of the residential areas of Schoten near Antwerp is an excellent example.

At the edge of the ornamental garden a vegetable garden and a garden with cut flowers have been laid out, surrounded by fan-trained fruit trees and bordering a formal rose garden. At the far end of the vegetable garden are various kinds of currant bushes. In front of the fruit trees is a delicate mixed border with blue, white and grey perennials, interplanted with some botanical roses. Scattered among the garden, which was designed by Jacques Wirtz, one of Flanders' most renowned landscape gardeners, are more fruit trees, including a quince (with beautiful pink blossoms in spring and large ochre fruits in autumn), medlars and cherries. In the enclosed ornamental garden immediately behind the terrace Wirtz has planted tall-stemmed fruit trees.

Integrated ornamental and utility gardens where vegetables and fruit are well represented are a typical feature of Flemish gardening.

Mr and Mrs Van Noten, who have retired after a

Few people are aware that many of the topiaries for which French and English gardens are renowned were imported from Flanders. In many old gardens these sculptured box and yew hedges, our version of Japanese bonsai, can still be seen. Topiaries have now become fashionable again, and as with all fashions the results are not always satisfactory. The subdued, almost meditative atmosphere of the Dedeyne garden in Waregem (above) and the exuberant shapes in a garden in Knokke (below), designed by landscape gardener Piet Blanckaert, are two totally different examples of topiary gardens. The topiaries of Mrs Van Glabbeek in Kapellen (right) tell their own story.

had to find a new home for the topiaries – yews trimmed in the shape of a horse, a squirrel and a teddy-bear – she had grown with so much care. These figures now grace the garden of Mr and Mrs van Glabbeek in Kapellen near Antwerp, who have become quite passionate about this type of ornamental gardening.

Some of us may think that sculptured hedges are decidedly banal. And so they are – to a certain extent. But in the proper environment they have an irresistible charm.

The landscape gardener Jacques Wirtz endeavoured to recreate the atmosphere of a rectory garden when he restored the garden of the Old Rectory in Kapellen, now a museum.

The layout is modelled on a Renaissance design with regular boxwood beds around a circular water basin of volcanic rock. The beds have been planted with a variety of old-fashioned perennials, including irises, catmint (*Nepeta*), lavender, peonies, lungwort (*Pulmonaria*) and lady's mantle (*Alchemilla mollis*), recalling the days when priests belonged to the local elite and exchanged plants with like-minded gardening enthusiasts.

In order to counterbalance the effect of the imposing church at the far end of the garden a great many trees and shrubs were planted to create a green canopy. Two arbours were constructed, both now completely overgrown. The garden is surrounded on all sides by walls and fan-trained trees, which contributes to its private and intimate character.

The need to isolate gardens from their surroundings is a permanent feature of Flemish gardening history. One of the reasons is, of course, the absence of mountains and valleys in this flat country, making it difficult to integrate landscape and garden. What is even more important is that in a densely populated region like Flanders, where space is scarce and people live

close together, gardens tend to be relatively small. In the new housing developments near towns and villages putting up some kind of partition is often a necessary first step when gardens are laid out. The Flemish jealously guard their privacy and, unlike the Dutch, they prefer to keep the more intimate details of their lives hidden from the eyes of the world.

Jacques Wirtz has incorporated that sense of privacy and seclusion in his distinctive design for the garden of a modern house in a residential area of Kapellen. A hornbeam hedge separates the garden from the street. A group of beeches at the rear helps to screen it off from the rest of the world. To match the appearance of the white-painted house Wirtz created an unadorned, Oriental-type garden with large lawns and two grassy knolls on either side of the entrance which are repeated by trimmed box and yew shrubs and rhodo-

The Van Der Elst garden in Kapellen, designed more than 25 years ago by Jacques Wirtz, still looks remarkably modern. At a time when people want to convince us that the quality of a garden depends on its being adorned with all kinds of pots, statuettes and benches, the almost Oriental simplicity of this garden proves that good landscape gardening does not require such fashionable embellishments.

dendrons. Outside the dining room a square plot was planted with catalpas filtering the sunlight; the plot is lined with cherry and apple trees flowering beautifully in spring.

A RESTRUCTURED LANDSCAPE

It is actually rather surprising that gardening has seen such a remarkable revival in Flanders since the seventies, at a time when building activities leading to ribbon developments and new housing projects on the edge of towns and villages have done irreparable damage to the Flemish countryside.

The Flemish have always been keen builders. This, together with the absence of proper town planning and the almost proverbial skill and ingenuity with which the average Fleming manages to evade the few existing regulations, has had dire consequences for the Flemish countryside. Thousands of acres of open space, precious nature reserves, woods and fields and historical towns and villages have fallen prey to the Flemish craze for property development.

Occasionally this attitude has actually benefited the owners of gardens: walls and hedges sometimes shelter private worlds that could never have existed if more stringent planning regulations had been in force and if people showed more respect for our natural heritage.

Most of the lots on new housing developments are small, however, and gardening budgets are tight. Coupled with the average Fleming's obsession with tidiness and his innate dislike of disorder, this has produced gardens that often consist of little more than a tiny lawn with a few unimaginative, carefully raked flowerbeds planted with annuals, preferably brightly coloured. Even more awful are pebble-strewn front gardens containing a single conifer or three silver birches that are pruned at frequent intervals. Fortunately this kind of lifeless desert is gradually becoming rarer.

Another and better approach is that chosen by Luc Meerts for his garden on a housing estate just outside Hasselt. Mr Meerts, an arts teacher, has here given full expression to his sense of colour and shape. Helped by his remarkable knowledge of plants he has created an exceptional garden, planted with perennials, on a plot of just one fifth of an acre. It is a superb example of the new type of popular gardening that has come into vogue in our days. Mr Meerts' garden leaves no doubt that its owner is a gardening enthusiast who has collected hundreds of rare plants. Unlike his illustrious predecessors from the sixteenth and nineteenth centuries, however, he does not select his plants for their rarity or exoticism but for their shape and colour, allowing him to create a harmonious whole.

I encountered another example of the creative use of limited space in a new housing development in Kortrijk. Here, the landscape gardener Paul Deroose created a splendid garden on a tiny plot belonging to a house in the cottage style so beloved by the Flemish. Deroose used an existing hornbeam hedge as the basis for his design. At the back of the house a large terrace was made, enclosed on two sides by the walls of the house and by tall hornbeams on its other two sides. In the middle is a formal pond and along the edges are several beds planted with flowers, shrubs and climbers. A large opening in the hedge gives access to a second enclosed garden, a square grassy space surrounded by hornbeam and fan-trained lime trees.

A FONDNESS FOR KITSCH

The simplicity of this garden, as pure as the faith of the American Shakers, starkly contrasts with the banality that is another permanent feature of Flemish gardening. Gardens in Flanders are often cluttered with the most diverse ornaments, ranging from old butter casks to rejected toilet bowls to car tires painted white and

This garden in Bruges, designed by Paul Deroose at the end of the sixties, illustrates what he had written some years earlier: 'The successful use of trimmed shapes, which are still largely taboo in Belgium, is evidence of maturity in the field of landscape gardening.'

an English cottage, is a rather formal garden structured by hornbeam and holly hedges. Entering the garden at the back of the house, however, you are thrilled by a magnificent border planted with perennials along the side of a large lawn and fronting an equally magnificent green hornbeam hedge. From early spring until late autumn the border, laid out and cared for by Mrs De Boungne herself, is a riot of flowers. The dominating colours of this sunny border are yellow, white, blue and grey.

Eva Fabry's garden in Kapellen is a horticultural delight, which is not surprising, considering that she is the senior guide of the famous Kalmthout Arboretum. There is even a unique specimen of *Crataegus tanacetifolia*, a beautiful white-flowered hawthorn with greyish leaves and large autumn fruit. Until recently it was the only specimen of this tree (which originally came from Turkey) in Western Europe. All hawthorns of this variety now growing in Belgium and Holland have come from this tree! Other gems are a fine pseudolarix, several ornamental apple trees, a superb *Prunus virginiana*, varieties of witch hazel, hydrangea and viburnum, and various kinds of perennials and ground cover for the shaded garden. Next to the terrace is a special corner with fragrant sunplants.

Although this garden is clearly the creation of a gardening enthusiast with an exceptional knowledge of plants ('plants are the main thing', Ms Fabry says), it is vibrant with life and a delightful place to stay.

The renewed interest in gardening may sometimes make people forget that a garden is not just a collection of plants. Gardens need to be structured. What is known as a wild garden, a concept enjoying some popularity today, is really a contradiction in terms. Gardens are by definition an environment created by man to be cultivated daily.

Structuring may be limited to a minimum, as in the garden of the Vuylsteke family in Eksaarde. Jul Vuylsteke is an artist who uses his garden and the surrounding meadows, lined with willows and mixed hedgerows, as one of his principal sources of inspiration. The luxuriant flower garden in front of the house, blending perfectly with the rural environment and matching the style of the seventeenth-century farmhouse, has a very 'natural' appearance, as if nature has been given free rein, but it is unmistakably a human creation. Its natural aspect derives mainly from its many unsophisticated, old-fashioned plants, including hydrangeas, geraniums, roses, foxglove and various kinds of hellebore. But the garden also contains many rare species carefully selected for their colour, shape of leaves and height. The arrangement is balanced by an old pear tree and some strategically placed shrubs and hedges, including even some trimmed box hedges, which at first seem a surprising element. They go perfectly with this type of garden, however, and were in fact often used in the past.

Mrs Pattyn's garden in Boutersem used to be sadly neglected, but in the space of just a few years she managed to change it into a flowery paradise containing several borders planted with perennials, each a different colour. In the lower part of the garden is a large pond with 'natural' plants like gunnera, butterbur, irises and water lilies. In spring thousands of wild daffodils flower here, as well as other bulbous plants. There are no 'geometric' lines in this garden, but hedges and paths create a clear structure so that it can be enjoyed even in winter. Like her eighteenth- and nineteenth-century predecessors Mrs Pattyn intends to build a large orangery.

Many of these gardens are representative of the picturesque style referred to earlier – classical, regular shapes near the house and a more natural, picturesque

At first Régine Verhaeghe from Winksele near Leuven simply wanted to grow flowers in her garden to help her with her hobby, flower-arranging. But now she is arranging flowers on a grand scale – her garden is one huge flower composition. The pictures show a blue border with some yellow and white interspersed.

atmosphere further along. But they are also reminiscent of the traditional farm gardens and the slightly more formal rectory gardens of the past. In addition, they are illustrative of the Flemish gardener's devotion to refinement and detail, rather than to the harmony and grandeur which are so characteristic of French and Italian gardens.

The Flemish gardening heritage is clearly in need of reappraisal. The almost proverbial modesty of the Flemish may well be the reason why such a reappraisal has not yet been forthcoming.

The luxuriant flower garden of the Vuylsteke family in Eksaarde is a perfect match for its rural environment and the seventeenth-century farmhouse. It looks very 'natural', as if nature has been given free rein, but it is unmistakably a human creation. Its natural aspect derives mainly from its many unsophisticated, 'old-fashioned' plants, such as foxglove.

227

Mrs Pattyn's romantic garden in
Boutersem is a horticulturalist's
dream. Near the house is a formal
flower garden, but further away,
past the large pond (right), you
come to an almost virgin piece of
nature with thousands of wild
daffodils and other bulbs. The pond
itself has been lavishly planted with
water lilies, irises, butterbur and
many other aquatic plants that seem
free to grow where they like. The
natural aspect of the garden,
however, is the result of years of
hard work and daily care. Gardens
are by definition an environment
created by man to be cultivated
daily.

228

A cobbled road linking two villages, Wannegem and Lede. The plain countryside is unassuming and peaceful. The wooden windmill even suggests a degree of poverty. But appearances are deceptive. A short distance away, beyond the mill, is Wannegem-Lede Castle. This building from 1785 is an imitation of the Petit Trianon in Versailles. Flanders is full of such surprising discoveries, although much has been destroyed. Large parts of the countryside have been sacrificed to new housing and many towns have had their hearts torn out. Fortunately, some superb historical buildings and monuments have been preserved, allowing people to communicate with the past and to enjoy beautiful things.

231